D1606897

CARRIER WAR

CARRIER WAR
AVIATION ART OF WORLD WAR II

Paul Stillwell

FRIEDMAN/FAIRFAX

A FRIEDMAN/FAIRFAX BOOK

© 2002 by Michael Friedman Publishing Group, Inc.

Please visit our website: www.metrobooks.com

All rights reserved. No part of this publication may be reproduced, stored in a retrieval
system, or transmitted, in any form or by any means, electronic, mechanical, photocopying,
recording, or otherwise, without prior written permission from the publisher.

Library of Congress Cataloging-in-Publication Data available upon request.

ISBN 1-58663-309-0

Editor: Nathaniel Marunas and Betsy Beier
Art Director: Kevin Ullrich
Photography Editor: Jami Ruszkai
Production Manager: Michael Vagnetti

Color separations by Fine Arts Repro House Co., Ltd.
Printed in Singapore by KHL Printing Co Pte Ltd

1 3 5 7 9 10 8 6 4 2

Distributed by Sterling Publishing Company, Inc.
387 Park Avenue South
New York, NY 10016
Distributed in Canada by Sterling Publishing
Canadian Manda Group
One Atlantic Avenue, Suite 105
Toronto, Ontario, Canada M6K 3E7
Distributed in Australia by
Capricorn Link (Australia) Pty, Ltd.
P.O. Box 704, Windsor, NSW 2756 Australia

Dedication

This book is dedicated to the memory of Vice Admiral Don Engen. He was a superb pilot and skilled administrator. Even more important, he was a great human being. He possessed the knack of being able to meet someone for the first time and make that person feel like his lifelong friend. He cared about people.

The publisher gratefully acknowledges the many talented artists who allowed their work to be included in these pages:

C.S. Bailey
Robert Bailey
Brian Bateman
Robert Benny
Mark Churms
James Dietz
William F. Draper
C.G. Evers
Tom Freeman
Mitchell Jamieson
Craig Kodera
Tom Lea
Albert K. Murray
William S. Phillips
Hugh Polder
John D. Shaw
Dwight C. Shepler
Thomas C. Skinner
R.G. Smith
Stan Stokes
Robert Taylor
Nicolas Trudgian
Ted Wilbur
Keith Woodcock

Acknowledgments

One of the real pleasures of putting this book together was to be involved with the work of longtime friends. Artist R.G. Smith, for example, did the cover painting for my first book. He was as modest and unassuming as he was talented, and his passing in 2001 left behind a host of admirers. In 1988, artist Bill Phillips and I spent three weeks together in the Persian Gulf to document the U.S. Navy's role in the tanker war then in progress between Iran and Iraq. In that time we visited ten different ships; Bill was a great shipmate and traveling companion. Tom Freeman did the cover art for this book and a number of paintings inside. Our association goes way back, as does my admiration for his skill in depicting ships and the water on which they operate. Ted Wilbur responded in friendly, enthusiastic fashion when asked for copies of his paintings to be used in the book.

Three authors of books on aircraft carriers were kind enough to read portions of this book's manuscript and provide helpful suggestions. Tom Hone, Bob Cressman, and Tim Wooldridge collectively have a most impressive knowledge of carriers and their evolution. Cressman shared a great photo from his collection of the first carrier, the *Yorktown*. Two other authors I have known for many years, Clark Reynolds and Norman Polmar, wrote classic books that I used for source material. Reynolds' *The Fast Carriers* is the best book I know of on American carrier operations in the Pacific in World War II. Ed Stafford and Steve Ewing, both of whom have chronicled the exploits of the legendary USS *Enterprise,* have extended kindnesses in past years that contributed to this book. Mac Greeley, for years a coworker at the U.S. Naval Institute, provided useful insights on artist Tom Lea. Marion Gilliland, whose grandfather and my father were shipmates many years ago, is the world's foremost expert on the work of portrait artist Albert K. Murray. Charlie Engen provided a number of photos from his father's aviation career, and John Fry contributed one from his book on the *Saratoga*. Dr. Ray Lewis supplied a copy of a Tom Freeman painting of the old *Saratoga* from his personal collection. And John Lundstrom, the sort of friend everyone would like to have, has been a frequent source of knowledge and encouragement.

Editorial Director Nathaniel Marunas skillfully leads a wonderful team at Barnes & Noble Publishing. I am grateful to him and his colleagues both for their professional contributions and their habitual friendliness. It was a pleasure to work once again with editor Betsy Beier and designer Kevin Ullrich. Betsy's contribution was in asking the probing questions and introducing the changes necessary to make the text clearer and more accurate; Kevin's handiwork is evident throughout the pages of this very attractive book. Finally, Jami Ruszkai has been unfailingly cheerful and resourceful in rounding up both the artwork and photographs that constitute the heart of the book.

Finally, I appreciate the great support from my family. Sons Joseph, Robert, and James are a perpetual source of pride. And my wife Karen has been patient and understanding during the time the book took me away from other activities.

Contents

Introduction

Fast and Furious, by artist Stan Stokes, depicts the first carrier air strike in naval history. Seven Sopwith Camels, each carrying two fifty-pound (23kg) bombs, were launched on July 19, 1918, by the British carrier *Furious* to attack German zeppelin sheds.

Seagoing aviation in the U.S. Navy began with primitive tests by pilot Eugene Ely, who worked for Glenn Curtiss, manufacturer of the service's first aircraft. As described by author Norman Polmar in his masterful book *Aircraft Carriers*, on November 13, 1910, sailors in the crew of the light cruiser *Birmingham* spent a Sunday building an eighty-three-foot (25m) wooden platform that stretched from the ship's bridge to the bow. The next day the cruiser hoisted aboard a Curtiss-built biplane, and that afternoon, as the *Birmingham* was under way in Hampton Roads, Virginia, Ely's fifty-horsepower plane took off. The aircraft's undercarriage dipped into the water for a moment, but it kept moving and landed two and a half miles (4km) away. The following month, Curtiss began training Lieutenant Theodore G. Ellyson at Hammondsport, New York. Ellyson was the U.S. Navy's first aviator.

On January 18, 1910, Ely achieved another first when he landed a plane on a 120-foot- (37m) long wooden platform erected on the stern of the armored cruiser *Pennsylvania*, which was anchored in San Francisco Bay. His plane was stopped upon landing by a series of cross-deck lines held down by sandbags; the lines caught hooks on the underside of Ely's plane—a crude forerunner of the arresting-wire system used on aircraft carriers today. Captain C.F. Pond of the *Pennsylvania* waxed positively ecstatic over the event: "This is the most important landing of a bird since the dove flew back to the Ark."

In Europe, the British were pursuing a parallel course of action, slightly behind the Americans. In the winter of 1911, Lieutenant Charles R. Samson flew a biplane off a wooden ramp situated on the bow of the battleship *Africa*. Later that year the Royal Navy commissioned the light cruiser *Hermes* to serve as a host ship for naval aviation operations and Samson continued his experiments. Britain officially established the Royal Naval Air Service on July 1, 1914, one month before World War I erupted on the European continent. During that war, planes operated mostly in support of ground troops and in raids on land targets. In August 1914, Samson and fellow British fliers became temporarily ground-based in Belgium to fly reconnaissance missions and combat patrols in support of Royal Marines who were fighting on land. The British installed aircraft facilities on a number of merchant ships for use as seaplane carriers during the war. From 1915 to 1917, Commander Samson was in command of a small force of converted ships whose seaplanes conducted raids in the Mediterranean and the Red Sea. Samson became Britain's top naval aviator of World War I.

While Ely's plane had wheels on the undercarriage, many of the early naval aircraft, including the first plane Curtiss built for the Navy, were equipped with pontoons and intended to operate from the water. Seaplanes were deployed to drop bombs on German zeppelin bases in an effort to reduce the threat that bomb-laden airships posed to Britain. The *Ark Royal*, intended as a merchant ship, was converted during construction to serve as a seaplane tender and transport. Polmar describes her as "the first ship fully converted for aircraft duties." She provided aviation services in the Mediterranean during the war.

The first aircraft carrier in the Royal Navy was HMS *Furious*. As Clark Reynolds points out in his superb book *The Fast Carriers*, the British had been disappointed by the performance of their battle cruisers in the 1916 dreadnought slugfest in the Battle of Jutland. Aerial reconnaissance, they hoped, would give them more opportunities to spot the enemy and bring about surface gunnery action. As with all of the early aviation ships, the *Furious* began her life as something else—in this case, a battle cruiser. She was originally designed to mount two 18-inch guns, one forward and one aft. Instead, the ship was completed with a hangar and flight deck forward, and an 18-inch gun aft. When the *Furious* joined the fleet in July 1917, she could launch planes but not recover them; they had to land ashore or in the sea. At first the ship was half carrier and half battle cruiser. Though not really effective in either role, the *Furious* represented a significant stage in warship evolution.

Late that year she went in for another dockyard alteration, this time to add a landing platform at the stern. But she still had problems. The amidships superstructure upset the air currents surrounding the carrier, making landings treacherous for the pilots brave enough to attempt them. So, although she had flight decks at both ends, she was limited to launching planes. On July 19, 1918, the *Furious* launched a successful strike against zeppelin sheds at Tondern, Germany, on the North Sea. But despite her successes, with no way to recover planes, the ship was of limited use as a carrier and operated as a balloon tender the rest of the war. She would be rebuilt several more times during the remainder of her career.

The British undertook still another conversion project in 1916 when they bought an incomplete Italian passenger ship, renamed her *Argus*, and installed a flight deck atop her hull. Unlike the *Furious*, nothing protruded above the level of the *Argus's* deck to interfere with flight operations; she bore a strong resemblance to the American *Langley*, which came along in the early 1920s. Another step in the move towards sea-based warplanes was the introduction of the Sopwith Cuckoo, the first torpedo-carrying plane to operate from an aircraft carrier. The first squadron of Cuckoos went aboard the *Argus* in October 1918, just a few weeks before the end of World War I; too late to take part in combat.

The first ship of any nation designed as an aircraft carrier was HMS *Hermes*, which took the name of the light cruiser that had been involved in previous aviation development. Construction began in January 1918 and she was launched in September 1919. Because the war had ended and with it the immediate requirement for combat service, she was not completed until July 1923, a year after the first American carrier went into commission. The new *Hermes* was the first ship to look like the type we have come to know as an aircraft carrier. She had a flat flight deck for the launching and recovery of planes, and to starboard she had what has come to be known as the "island," a superstructure that includes the bridge, mast, and smokestack. The *Hermes* was nearly 600 feet long (183m) and had a displacement of 10,850 tons (9,843t).

In the United States during the period between world wars, battleships were still by far the preeminent ships of the fleet, as they were in all the major navies of the world. The battleship would keep this distinction until the 1941 attack on Pearl Harbor, which dramatically changed international perspectives. Individuals with an interest in aviation sought to build on the early demonstrations by Eugene Ely, but most of the emphasis was on operating seaplanes. There were a few experiments with shipborne aircraft, primarily to serve as eyes in the sky to seek out enemy ships and then to direct naval gunfire when the enemy was found. Once battleships achieved the capability to fire beyond the visual horizon, the ships' crews needed a way to see how close to the target their projectiles were falling so they could make corrections accordingly. To this end, capital ships in both Britain and the United States erected flying-off platforms on top of turret guns from which spotting planes were launched.

These, like the early carrier planes, could not land back aboard ship and thus had severely limited utility.

Japan began to explore naval aviation in 1912, not long after the United States and Britain got involved. Clark Reynolds has written of First Lieutenant Yozo Kaneko, who put on a demonstration for the Emperor during a naval review in the autumn of 1912. As an airplane and airship flew overhead, he landed his seaplane near the Emperor's flagship. To increase the nation's aviation experience, Japan sent young naval officers to France and America for flight instruction. One of those trained in the United States was Lieutenant Chikuhei Nakajima, who subsequently established an aircraft company that bore his name and produced many of the planes Japan used in World War II. After conducting some experiments with seaplanes, in December 1919 Japan began construction on the small aircraft carrier *Hosho*, or "flying Phoenix." Like the British *Hermes*, she had been designed for this purpose rather than being converted from an existing ship. She also had a primitive island structure, though it was later removed to make landings easier for pilots.

The *Hosho* was finished in December 1922, a few months after the American conversion carrier *Langley* but before the British *Hermes*. She was thus the world's first ship to be completed as a built-for-the-purpose aircraft carrier. The ship began flight operations in early 1923; she could accommodate a total of twenty-one planes. As more aircraft carriers joined the Imperial Japanese Navy over succeeding years, the *Hosho* became principally a training ship. She did participate in combat operations in the Sino-Japanese War and was part of the Japanese force engaged in the Battle of Midway, though not part of the principal strike force. Unlike her bigger, newer counterparts, the *Hosho* survived World War II. After the war, she brought her country's soldiers home from China. Her end came in 1947 when she was turned to scrap at Osaka, Japan.

Even before World War I ended, events had begun to work against British naval aviation. In 1917 German Gotha bombers attacked London and sowed a crop of destruction. German bombs killed and wounded British citizens, and they demolished cities. Understandably, it was not the sort of situation that the British nation, particularly its politicians, could afford to ignore. On April 1, 1918, Britain amalgamated the Royal Flying Corps and the Royal Naval Air

Service to form a new organization named the Royal Air Force. The United States, by comparison, did not take the step of creating a separate air force until a generation later, in 1947. Even then, the United States took a different tack in that it hatched its new service from what had been the air component of the U.S. Army. It did not do away with the separate air arms of the Navy, Marine Corps, and Coast Guard, and therein lay a huge difference. Because Britain's new Fleet Air Arm, so named in 1924, was not part of the Navy per se, the effect on seagoing aviation in the Royal Navy over the next two decades was deleterious. By the time the Fleet Air Arm was put back into the Royal Navy in 1939, Britain had long since lost the lead in carrier aviation that it had enjoyed twenty years earlier. It would never again be number one.

Three historians—Thomas C. Hone, Norman Friedman, and Mark D. Mandeles—have addressed the subject in great detail in a book titled *American and British Aircraft Carrier Development: 1919–1941*. Part of the problem facing naval progress was a phenomenon that swept the leading military nations around the end of World War I and had considerable influence in the years immediately afterward. This was the idea that bombing aircraft had made armies and navies obsolete. It became known as the doctrine of strategic bombing. As this theory went, when nations went to war, all they had to do was send their planes over to bomb enemy soldiers and sink enemy warships. In the new Royal Air Force, primacy went to the bomber advocates, because the strategic bombing theory seemed to offer some very attractive benefits. It was a way of killing the enemy without exposing ground troops to hazard and without making expensive investments in warships. Though strategic bombing would have its uses in various conflicts, as events of the past eighty years have demonstrated, wars could not be won aerial bombing alone.

In the United States, Army Brigadier General Billy Mitchell garnered a great deal of public attention by preaching the gospel of strategic bombing. The media-savvy flier staged publicity stunts to try to prove his point. He arranged for tests in which Army planes bombed obsolete warships. In June 1921, his bombers sank the former German battleship *Ostfriesland*, and his planes did away with obsolete American battleships too. But these ships were not maneuvering, nor did they have antiaircraft guns to defend themselves.

Still, Mitchell's claims were not entirely without merit. As bombers and torpedo planes became ever more capable in the years ahead, surface warships did become increasingly vulnerable, especially since dive-bombing tactics developed faster than antiaircraft gunnery. The remedy, however, was not to do away with surface ships. As time passed, a number of solutions were found, including defending ships with fighter planes that could oppose the bombers, improving antiaircraft guns, inventing projectiles that exploded near enemy aircraft without having to make direct hits, and developing a device called radar that could detect incoming planes at considerable distances.

Coincident with the rise of the theory of strategic bombing was the change in attitudes toward naval power in the wake of World War I. An international gathering to effect naval disarmament was convened in 1921 by U.S. Secretary of State Charles Evans Hughes. The nations of the world had recently completed a conflict then described as "the war to end all wars." The new American president, Warren Harding, pledged that the nation would return to prewar "normalcy." In an effort to avoid the costs associated with a continuing naval arms race, the Washington Naval Conference of 1921–22 negotiated on a number of issues, primarily focusing on limiting the growth of battleships. The Americans had an advantage in that negotiation. Having intercepted and decrypted the messages that Japan was sending to its envoys in the United States, the Americans knew just what limits Japan would be willing to accept. The Washington Naval Treaty, signed in February 1922, established limits on capital ship tonnage for the United States, Britain, Japan, France, and Italy. The result was the scrapping of some existing battleships, the cancellation of construction on others, and a ten-year moratorium on the building of new capital ships.

Another provision of the treaty specified tonnage limits for the construction of aircraft carriers. The United States and Britain were each permitted 135,000 tons (122,472t) for carriers, and Japan got 81,000 tons (73,483t). Included in the treaty at the suggestion of the British, was the stipulation that the three nations could each convert two capital ships then under construction to carriers. The ships that resulted from this treaty were to play important roles in each nation's development of carrier aviation in the 1920s and 1930s. These first treaty carriers would also be used in combat during World War II.

USS *Langley* (CV-1)/(AV-3)

In the early part of the twentieth century, the U.S. Navy used a number of seagoing colliers to supplement the work of coaling stations. In April 1913, the Mare Island Navy Yard in Vallejo, California, completed the new collier *Jupiter*. The ship's first commanding officer was Commander Joseph Mason Reeves, who was known as "Billy Goat" because of his goatee. He would play an important role in the ship's later career.

During her first few years of service, the *Jupiter* refueled other vessels while alongside at anchor. The tall derricks rising from her hull were used to move the coal to other ships and then drop it on deck. During World War I, the *Jupiter* at times took leave of her coaling duties to deliver other types of cargo to the war zone. In early 1919 she brought American war veterans home from France.

In the meantime, the British had demonstrated a number of benefits to be derived from sea-based aviation. Accordingly, In July 1919 the U.S. Congress authorized the conversion of the *Jupiter* into the first American aircraft carrier. She was chosen because her roomy holds could be transformed into a hangar and storage spaces. At the Norfolk Navy Yard near Hampton Roads, Virginia, the tall derricks came off, and Erector set–like girders sprouted in their place. The girders enclosed a hangar deck for parking airplanes, while on top of the

hangar, a flight deck took shape. The changes earned her a new nickname in the fleet: "The Covered Wagon." Retractable masts for the flying of signal flags poked through the flight deck, and the smokestacks, located near the stern, could be pivoted to horizontal position so as not to interfere with flight operations. She was 542 feet (165m) long, 65 feet (20m) wide, and displaced 11,500 tons (10,433t). By comparison, today's nuclear-powered super carriers are more than 1,000 feet (305m) long and displace more than 90,000 tons (81,647t) each.

With the new look came a new name, *Langley*, in honor of Samuel Pierpont Langley (1834–1906), a prominent physicist and astronomer who had done pioneering work in developing heavier-than-air craft. The ship was recommissioned as an aircraft carrier on March 20, 1922. Commander Kenneth Whiting, the USS *Langley*'s first executive officer and a man of vision and drive, was instrumental in ensuring that the new ship fulfilled her potential. The *Langley* became a floating test platform, pioneering the use of landing signal officers to guide incoming planes and cross-deck arresting wires, which have since become standard equipment on carriers. The ship also had fore-and-aft wires to keep incoming planes from swerving, but they proved unwieldy and were removed.

Jack Tate, one of the *Langley*'s first aviators, later explained what a novelty the ship was. He reported that in 1922 there were only 314 pilots in the Navy, and few knew how to fly planes with wheels, having been trained on seaplanes,

which have pontoons. On October 17, 1922, Lieutenant Commander Virgil Griffin piloted the first plane from the *Langley*'s flight deck; nine days later Lieutenant Commander Godfrey Chevalier accomplished the first landing when the ship was under way. Chevalier had little time to savor his triumph. He was killed in a plane crash the following month, a vivid demonstration of the perils of aviation.

In the years that followed, the *Langley* joined up with the Battle Fleet on the West Coast and demonstrated the ability to perform scouting roles for battleships and cruisers, which were considered the Navy's prime offensive weapons. Reeves, by now a rear admiral, commanded the aircraft squadrons in the fleet; among his innovations was to use carrier planes as weapons themselves, rather than mere observation craft. In war games, Reeves brought larger numbers of planes aboard the ship and cut down the interval between launches as a means of enhancing the ability to strike targets at sea. The *Langley* thus paved the way for the bigger and faster aircraft carriers of the future.

By 1937 the number of new carriers that had come into service had rendered the outmoded pioneer more or less obsolete. The forward part of her flight deck was removed and she was converted to a seaplane tender. In the early days of the war in the Pacific she operated as a mobile base for seaplanes around the Philippines. In February 1942, she was directed to deliver fighter planes to Java in the Dutch East Indies. On February 27, Japanese bombers damaged the ship so severely that she was unable to reach her destination. U.S. warships sank the *Langley* with gunfire and torpedoes, thus bringing to a close her nearly thirty years of varied, groundbreaking service.

OPPOSITE LEFT: The collier *Jupiter* with her original coaling rig.
OPPOSITE RIGHT: The *Jupiter* undergoes transformation into a carrier at Norfolk Navy Yard.
BELOW LEFT: The *Langley* with a load of planes on deck after she rejoined the fleet in her new role.
BELOW RIGHT: The conversion of the *Langley* to a seaplane tender had shorn her of the forward end of the flight deck.
LEFT: Joseph Mason Reeves as a rear admiral, his rank during the late 1920s, when he made important strides in the deployment of carriers as part of the Battle Fleet. The forward-looking Reeves graduated from the Naval Academy in 1894. He served in the battleship *Oregon* during the notable Battle of Santiago in the Spanish-American War of 1898. Later, in addition to the collier Jupiter, he commanded the cruiser *St. Louis* and battleships *Oregon* and *Delaware*. As a four-star admiral in the mid-1930s, Reeves commanded the Battle Force, and then the entire U.S. Fleet. After retiring in 1936, he was recalled to active duty and performed useful service up to 1945.

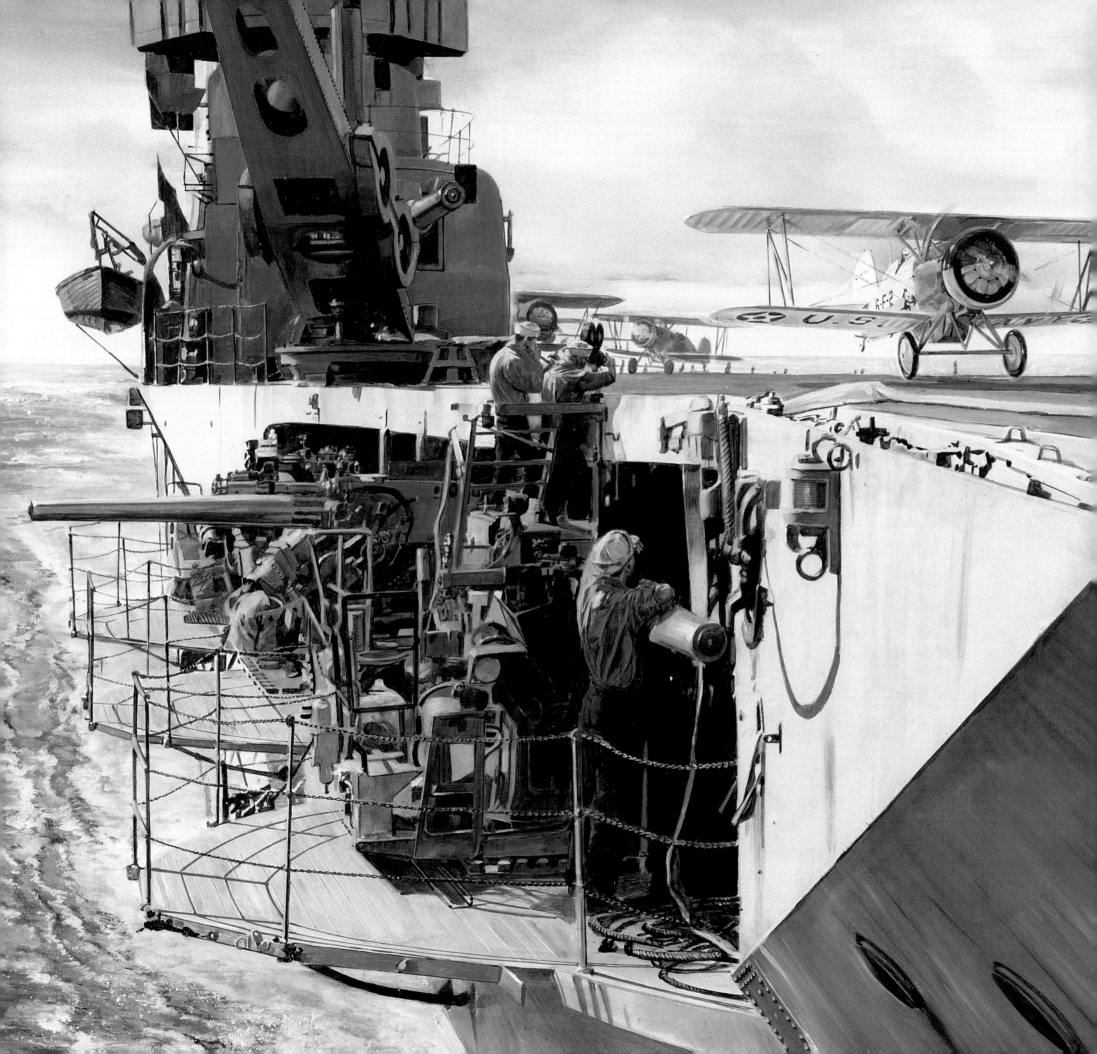

LEFT: In James Dietz's painting *Felix Leaves Sara*, a Boeing F4B fighter plane of Fighting Three (VF-3) is in the middle of her takeoff run from the flight deck of the carrier *Saratoga* in the mid-1930s. VF-3 was known as the "Felix the Cat" squadron because its insignia featured the cartoon character by that name. In the foreground are 5-inch antiaircraft guns.

ABOVE: This painting, *Aircraft Carrier Ranger 1934* by Thomas Skinner, shows the first American aircraft carrier built from the keel up for that purpose. She is depicted in the bustling Newport News Shipbuilding and Dry Dock Company in Virginia where she was built—the same shipyard that produces aircraft carriers for the U.S. Navy of the twenty-first century.

In same time period, two important developments took place within the U.S. Navy. The first was a reaction to the fuss stirred up by Billy Mitchell: the establishment of the Bureau of Aeronautics in 1921. A specialized organization, the Bureau of Aeronautics would oversee the design and procurement of new naval aircraft and aviation-related ships, and the training of aviation personnel. The first chief of the bureau was Rear Admiral William Moffett, who was so effective an advocate for naval aviation that he held the post for the next twelve years, until his death in the crash of the dirigible *Akron* in 1933. The second milestone was the commissioning in March 1922 of the USS *Langley*, the first U.S. aircraft carrier. (See pages 12–13.)

The Royal Navy did not have the benefit of a specialized naval aviation organization such as the Bureau of Aeronautics. The book by Hone, Friedman, and Mandeles provides manifold lessons on the law of unintended consequences. The British had cogent reasons for establishing a unified air service, but the results were particularly harmful for the seagoing portion of the Royal Air Force.

Tom Freeman's painting *Saratoga* shows one of the two aircraft carriers converted from battle cruisers as a result of the 1922 naval disarmament treaty. She and her sister *Lexington* proved to be test platforms for the development of carrier warfare and training platforms for many World War II naval aviators.

For one thing, the staff officers of the new Royal Air Force were primarily men from the Army rather than the Navy, and brought with them an emphasis on land-based bombers. When funds were short in the new post-disarmament climate, naval needs suffered. Further, the RAF hierarchy did not have a thorough understanding of the special requirements of operating aircraft at sea. The British naval aircraft that developed during the period between world wars were not as capable as their land-based counterparts. Because of limited aircraft capacity on board their carriers, the British sought versatility with multimission aircraft that, unfortunately, couldn't perform their missions as well as specialized planes. Thus they did not stack up well when it came time for combat in World War II. The problem was eventually solved during the war when British carriers were equipped with American naval warplanes.

In contrast, the U.S. Navy benefited from several factors that fostered the development of carrier aviation. In the mid-1920s, also in reaction to Billy Mitchell's push toward strategic bombing, President Calvin Coolidge directed lawyer-banker Dwight Morrow (future father-in-law of famed pilot Charles Lindbergh) to chair a board that examined the status of the nation's aviation practices. The board specifically rejected a unified air service on the British model, and it further recommended that aircraft carriers, other aviation-related ships, and naval air facilities ashore all be commanded by naval aviators or naval (air) observers. The latter recommendation was soon enacted into law and ensured that senior personnel involved with the aviation portion of the Navy would have an air-minded approach. One result of the new law was that a number of senior officers whose careers had involved surface ships such as battleships, cruisers, and destroyers now sought aviation training to qualify for carrier command. These newcomers included such World War II leaders as Ernest J. King, William F. Halsey, and John S. McCain, grandfather of the current senator from Arizona. They joined officers such as John Towers and Marc Mitscher, who had been aviators since early in their careers, to provide a solid backing for the use of aircraft with the fleet.

Another advantage of the U.S. setup was superior institutional structure. Hone, Friedman, and Mandeles have described the interlocking relationship among three separate entities: the Bureau of Aeronautics in Washington; the Naval War College in Newport, Rhode Island; and the fleet itself, which was largely based in southern California. Each year, war college personnel played simulated war games on the college floor, demonstrating the capabilities that aviation added. These concepts were tried out in the annual fleet problems that pitted teams of warships against each other in mock combat. In the late 1920s and early 1930s, these war games demonstrated that sea-based aircraft could do much more than just scout to detect an enemy and provide corrections for the battleships' gunfire. They could form an offensive force and attack with bombs and torpedoes, particularly as the technique of dive-bombing developed. After approaching targets in level flight, a bomber would push over into a steep dive that carried it down toward the target and thus provided for greater accuracy than the dropping of bombs from high altitude. Aircraft could also inflict damage by machine-gunning the targets.

In 1927 the United States commissioned its two large aircraft carriers, the *Lexington* and the *Saratoga*, which had been converted from battle cruisers as a result of the 1922 disarmament treaty. In 1929 the carriers were involved in a fleet problem that showed the effectiveness of aircraft in a mock attack on the Panama Canal. In February 1932 planes from the *Lexington* and *Saratoga* staged a simulated attack on the island of Oahu on a Sunday morning. The maneuver caught the defending Army aviators completely by surprise and served as an eerie precursor to the Japanese attack in December 1941. The United States realized that in a war with Japan it would probably have to combat land-based aircraft. With this in mind, planes were developed that could operate from a ship but still be comparable to those operating from ashore. Another considera-

tion was the development of fighter planes as part of carrier air groups. Fighters should be able to intercept incoming enemy planes and also serve as escorts for strike groups composed of bombers and torpedo planes.

A hampering factor throughout this period was the shortage of tonnage available for carriers because of the disarmament treaty. As a result, the first American aircraft carrier built from the keel up especially for that mission was a relatively small ship. She was the USS *Ranger*, with 14,500 tons (13,154t) displacement, compared with 33,000 tons (29,938t) each for the *Lexington* and *Saratoga*. She was commissioned in 1934 with Captain Arthur L. Bristol as the first commanding officer. She beefed up carrier numbers in the fleet but was a step backward in capability. The real advance came, ironically, as a result of the Depression that cast a pall over the country during much of the 1930s. In the 1920s the Republican administrations had cut back on naval expenditures and had not even built as many ships as the disarmament treaties (including one enacted in 1930) permitted. The new Democratic administration of President Franklin Roosevelt, who took office in 1933, continued this trend for a very short time. The National Industrial Recovery Act of 1933 authorized the use of Depression-relief funds to build new 20,000-ton (18,144t) carriers, the *Yorktown* and *Enterprise*. The 1934 Vinson-Trammell Act, which called for increased naval armaments, also had a salutary effect in building the fleet. The *Enterprise, Yorktown,* and their later near-sister *Hornet* were far more capable than the *Ranger* and represented a step forward in the evolution of carriers. All three were important in World War II, particularly in the tide-turning Battle of Midway in June 1942.

In Britain, where much pioneering work with carriers had been done because of the impetus posed by World War I, the Royal Navy got something of a break with the 1922 disarmament treaty. It was able to argue that a number of its early ships, comparable to the USS *Langley*, were really experimental ships and thus should not count against the tonnage limits imposed by the treaty. The tonnage limit, equal to that of the United States, allowed for six new carriers. The *Furious*, which had launched a combat strike against Germany in 1918, was again rebuilt; however, because of limited aircraft capacity, it was still not as capable as a new carrier designed for the mission. One remedy was to give her two flight decks, one atop the ship and another leading forward from the hangar

In *The Professionals*, James Dietz shows us Boeing F4B fighters warming up on the flight deck of the carrier *Lexington* in 1935. These are planes of Fighting Two, a squadron nicknamed "The Flying Chiefs" because most of the pilots were enlisted sailors who had undergone flight training. On the fuselage of each plane, below and forward of the pilot, is a chief petty officer insignia.

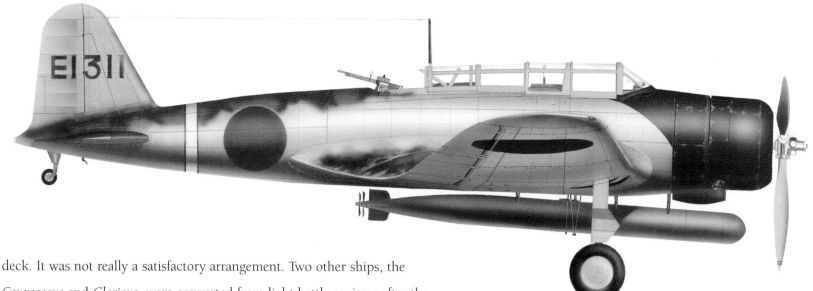

Kate, by C.S. Bailey depicts a Nakajima Type 97 carrier attack plane. The plane's nickname was one of a series of women's names that the Allies applied to enemy aircraft to facilitate rapid identification. The Japanese used Kates with devastating effect at Pearl Harbor. Some launched torpedoes; others dropped armor-piercing bombs, including the one that blew up the battleship *Arizona*.

deck. It was not really a satisfactory arrangement. Two other ships, the *Courageous* and *Glorious*, were converted from light battle cruisers after the conclusion of the 1922 treaty. Both were sunk by German naval forces soon after the beginning of World War II. Then, almost parallel with the United States, Britain built several large new carriers—*Ark Royal, Illustrious, Victorious, Formidable,* and *Indomitable*—that served in World War II. The *Ark Royal* had a key role in the eventual sinking of the German battleship *Bismarck* in 1941.

Britain's naval aviation continued to suffer as the 1930s progressed and the nation moved into World War II. The newer British carriers had armored flight decks to protect against land-based planes in Europe, smaller aircraft capacities than their American counterparts, and enclosed hangar decks. With the piston/ propeller engines of the era, the planes needed time to warm up before being launched. American carriers had hangar deck roller curtains that allowed for ventilation and below-decks warm-up; the British ships did not. Hone, Friedman, and Mandeles point up still other factors. For instance, in the Royal Air Force there was reluctance to use planes in support of ground troops, and thus Britain did not develop dive-bombing as well as the United States and Japan. In the 1930s, with war fast approaching, Britain rearmed itself with airplanes that were less capable than those of other nations; it didn't have sufficient resources to produce better aircraft in large numbers when they came along. The Swordfish torpedo biplanes on British carriers at the outset of war looked like relics from World War I, even though the Swordfish was a relatively new plane. It had been designed with a slow landing speed because of concern about the reliability of flight deck arresting wires. When the Fleet Air Arm moved from the RAF to

the Royal Navy in 1939, a handicap still persisted. The Navy got only the carrier planes and not the Coastal Command planes. The land-based Coastal Command planes were poorly equipped for antisubmarine patrol, and the *Courageous* was lost early in the war while trying to make up for shortages of antisubmarine aircraft.

Meanwhile, in Germany, Chancellor Adolf Hitler was growing ever more powerful. But, fortunately for the Allied navies in World War II, his ambitions outran sound planning. Hitler was working with his admirals to develop a balanced fleet that would be ready by 1945, when he intended to start a war. The fleet was to include aircraft carriers, the first of which being the 27,000-ton (24,494t) *Graf Zeppelin*. A shipyard in Kiel laid her keel in December 1936 and launched her partially completed hull in December 1938. But Hitler started war in September 1939, far ahead of his original plan. By that time the *Graf Zeppelin* was nearly ninety percent complete, and the intent was to commission her in the spring of 1940. In the meantime, however, Germany interrupted construction of the carrier and shifted its shipbuilding priority to U-boats. She was never finished and was eventually scuttled in 1945. The Germans also began construction of a second carrier, with the idea that lessons learned from the brief operation of the *Graf Zeppelin* could be incorporated into her design. The building of the second ship did not go far; the process was stopped in March 1940 and the beginning portion of the ship was scrapped.

In Japan, as in the United States during the inter-war period, the early British efforts with aircraft carriers served as examples. As Hone, Friedman, and Mandeles report, in November 1921, British aviation pioneer Sir William Forbes-Sempill headed a training mission to Japan that provided useful lessons for the country's Army and Navy aviation. One group of British pilots helped train their Japanese counterparts to land on Japan's new carrier, *Hosho*. Japan also followed the British practice of lowering newly landed aircraft into the hangar deck. (The Americans, by contrast, pushed their planes to the forward end of the flight deck to speed up the landing process.) After the disarmament treaty, the Japanese converted two planned gun ships—the battle cruiser *Akagi* and the battleship *Kaga*—to aircraft carriers comparable in size to their American counterparts. The battle cruiser *Amagi* was intended for conversion but was destroyed in the 1923 earthquake that ravaged Japan. The *Akagi* and *Kaga* gave the Imperial Japanese Navy a great deal of experience in operating aircraft at sea and developing the procedures that would be used in World War II. In addition, many Japanese wartime pilots developed their skills on board these two ships.

In 1927, following the lead of the Americans, the Japanese Navy established organizations that specialized in naval aviation: a Combined Naval Air Command and a Bureau of Aeronautics. In the ensuing years, the Japanese proceeded to construct carriers designed for that role from the outset: *Ryujo*, *Soryu*, and *Hiryu*.

In 1934 Japan officially renounced the disarmament treaties; its action was to take effect at the end of 1936. The move permitted its naval buildup to proceed at a pace unfettered by the limitations that the treaty had imposed for a decade and a half. In 1937 it began construction of two new large warships. In 1941, when the two 26,000-ton (23,587t) aircraft carriers, *Shokaku* and *Zuikaku*, joined the fleet, they were larger than the newest prewar American carriers. As Hone, Friedman, and Mandeles put it, "By mid-1941 the IJN had more carriers and better aircraft than any other navy in the world."

The Japanese had added to their strength in the inter-war period with a large contingent of land-based naval aircraft that could deliver bombs and torpedoes at long ranges, notably the planes that later acquired the nicknames "Nell" and "Betty." Like the Americans, the Japanese perfected dive-bombing techniques. They designed and built a hot new fighter, the Mitsubishi "Zero," which would become a truly formidable weapon in the early stages of World War II, and the "Val" dive-bomber. The "Kate" was a carrier-based attack plane that could serve as either a torpedo plane or a high-level bomber. One "Kate" dropped a bomb that wrecked the battleship *Arizona* at Pearl Harbor.

The Imperial Japanese Navy also had a rigorous aviation training program, as described by fighter ace Saburo Sakai in his memoir *Samurai!* The program took the cream of the cream of the crop and ran them through a training regimen so tough that all but the best and brightest fell by the wayside. These

C.S. Bailey's *Avenger* is a portrait of a Navy torpedo bomber used from 1942 onward by U.S. carriers in the Pacific. The Avenger carried a three-man crew and was capable of launching torpedoes or delivering bombs in a gliding attack rather than the steeper approach used by dive-bombers. The model of the Avenger built by Grumman was designated TBF; the General Motors version was TBM.

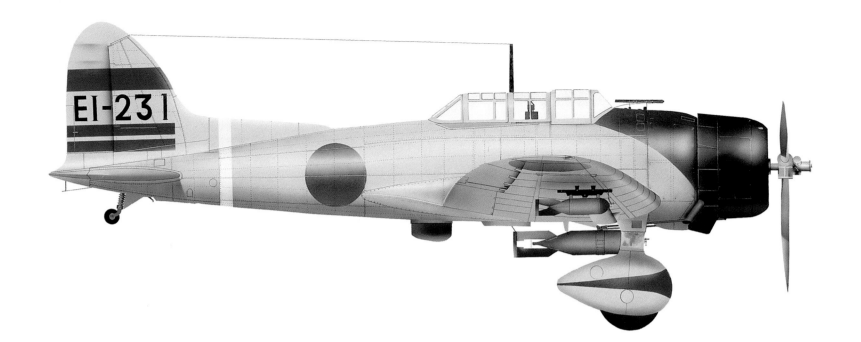

In *Val*, C.S. Bailey shows Japan's Type 99 carrier dive-bomber, which was used to attack ship and shore targets. In the raid on Pearl Harbor, attacking pilots hit airfields ashore to prevent fighters from rising up against the Japanese, and they also bombed ships in the harbor itself. A noteworthy recognition feature on this airplane is the fixed—rather than retractable—landing gear.

remaining aviators were extremely capable and provided an elite corps of fighting men who achieved much in the early days of the coming war. But the system was not able to replicate itself. Many of these top-notch fliers continued in combat until they were lost in action. They did not rotate back to training commands to pass on their skills, as did American pilots. Thus, when the best of the best were lost, their replacements were not nearly so capable.

From 1937 onward the Japanese engaged in a war they referred to as the "China Incident." This conflict provided combat experience for naval aviators and the crews of the carriers from which they operated. The war against China was part of an overall effort to create an empire known as the Greater East Asia Co-Prosperity Sphere. It was a plan for international conquest that would make Japan triumphant in the Western Pacific. But Japan was a country with limited natural resources, and thus it looked southward for sources of the tin, rubber, and petroleum it would need for the nourishment of its war machine. Increasingly, the government of Japan came to be ruled by militaristic elements, including General Hideki Tojo, who became Prime Minister in October 1941.

Japan had neither the resources nor the shipbuilding capacity to fight a prolonged naval war against the United States. The Japanese sent envoys to the United States in an attempt to work out some sort of modus vivendi, a

live-and-let-live approach that would allow Japan to retain the territories it had occupied in East Asia. For its part, the United States was seeking a way to intervene in the European war on behalf of Great Britain, which lost ally after ally as the German war machine achieved startling successes in Europe in 1939–40.

After the failure of negotiations with Japan led to the December 1941 attack on Pearl Harbor, the United States entered the conflict that had started with the German invasion of Poland in 1939. Lieutenant Commander Minoru Genda played a key role in developing Japanese carrier tactics and formations. As Clark Reynolds explains in *The Fast Carriers*, Genda, ironically, drew part of his inspiration from watching newsreel films of U.S. carriers operating together. It was Genda who planned the Pearl Harbor strike, an air raid that conclusively demonstrated the great strides carrier warfare had made in the two preceding decades. But in the months following the deadly strike, American carriers would trump the Japanese. U.S. industrial capacity was able to out-produce the Japanese and turn out a flood of carriers, both large and small. The mobility and striking power of those carriers made a major contribution to the eventual Allied victory. The pages that follow describe how the weapons developed and the lessons learned in the three decades leading up to World War II were put to devastating use.

A F6F Hellcat fighter warms up on the flight deck of the new carrier *Yorktown* in the spring of 1943. The pilot awaits his takeoff signal and an enlisted crewman on deck prepares to pull out a chock that blocks one wheel of the landing gear. Dozens of spectators look on from the superstructure of the ship.

Carrier War

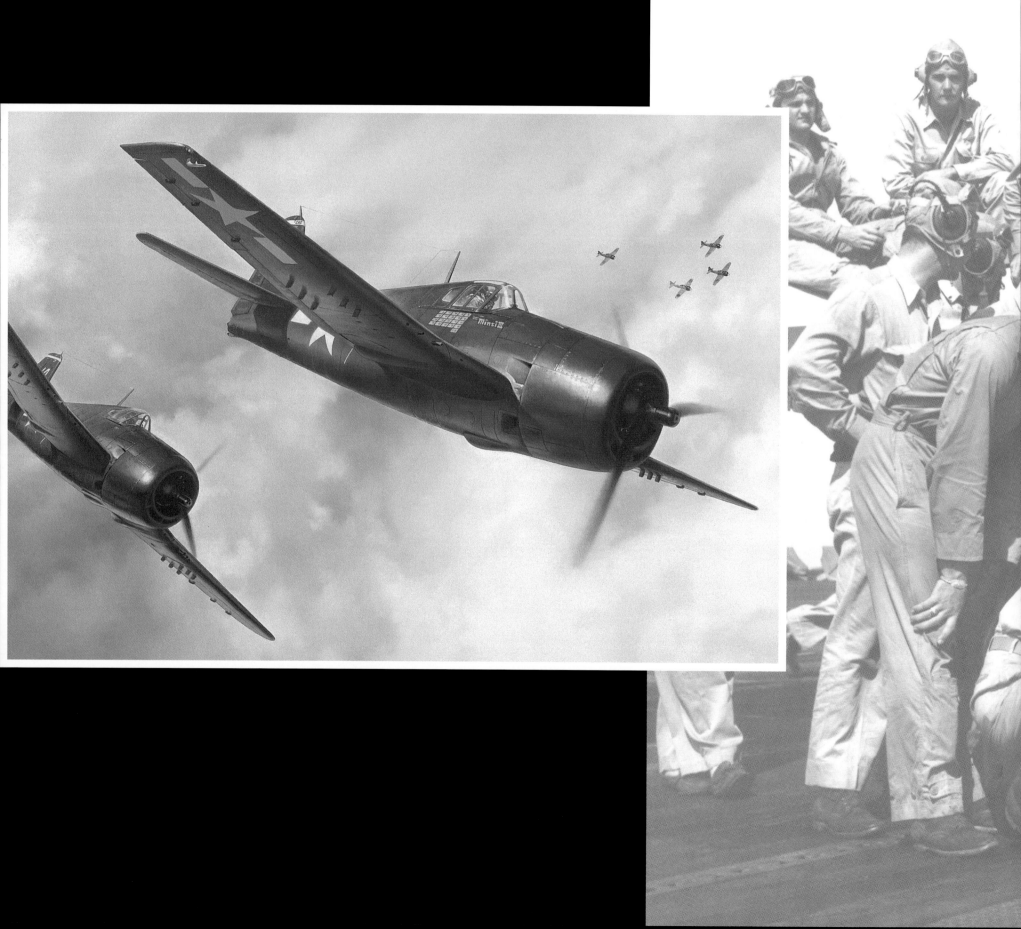

Moment of Truth

British Royal Navy

Keith Woodcock

IN THE SPRING OF 1940, THE BRITISH SENT PLANES, SHIPS, AND SOLDIERS TO AID IN THE defense of Norway against invasion by the fast-approaching Germans. Among the aircraft dispatched to the scene were Hawker Hurricane fighters of 263 Squadron, based at Bardufoss, north of the Arctic Circle. In early June, however, British forces had to evacuate so they would be ready for more pressing duty. But the Hurricanes didn't have enough range to fly all the way to England. Squadron Leader Bing Cross, commanding officer of 263, received orders to destroy the Hurricanes to prevent the Germans from capturing them. Cross had a better idea.

He and his pilots were determined to land the fighters on board the British carrier *Glorious* and thus keep them from the Germans' clutches. They put a 112-pound (51kg) bag of sand in the rear of each fuselage so the planes would not nose over when the pilots braked hard. This was the only alternative, because the planes had no arresting gear, nor had the pilots ever landed aboard aircraft carriers before. They conducted trials at Bardufoss until they were ready to try the maneuver at sea. *Moment of Truth* depicts Squadron Leader Cross as he approaches the stern of HMS *Glorious* on June 6, 1940, for his first trip aboard an aircraft carrier. He landed successfully, and eleven squadron mates followed after him.

Sadly, their triumph was short-lived. On June 8 the carrier and her escorting destroyers, *Acasta* and *Ardent*, came into contact with two surface raiders, the modern German battle cruisers, the *Scharnhorst* and the *Gneisenau*. The cruisers administered a pounding with their 11-inch (28cm) guns and sank the *Glorious* in little more than an hour. She had originally been a battle cruiser herself, later converted to a carrier in the 1920s. But, in the end, her armor was insufficient to protect her and she perished, along with the destroyers and the fighter planes and pilots so recently embarked in Norway. The only Hurricane pilot who survived was Cross, who spent seven days in a lifeboat before being rescued. For their part, the two German capital ships were damaged off Norway by British torpedoes, but both were repaired and returned to service.

28 SWORDFISH ATTACK AT TARANTO

Swordfish Attack at Taranto

British Royal Navy

Robert Taylor

THE FIRST SUCCESSFUL CARRIER ACTION OF WORLD WAR II GREW OUT OF THE increasingly tenuous situation that faced the Allies as 1940 advanced. In the spring of that year, the German war machine crunched through Western Europe. France fell, and shortly after, Italy entered the war on the Axis side. As a result, Great Britain found itself essentially alone, no longer able to count on French naval aid in the Mediterranean and faced with a threat from Italy's fleet. The major Italian warships were stationed at Taranto, a port city near the bottom of the foot of the boot-shaped nation.

Admiral Andrew Cunningham, British naval commander in the Mediterranean, was spoiling for a fight because the Italian warships, even in port, constituted a threat to Cunningham's fleet and forced him to tie down corresponding numbers of British warships to the region to counter them. But the Italians chose not to take the bait and remained bottled up. When the Italians wouldn't come out, Cunningham decided to send in a swarm of aircraft to attack them. In so doing, he was putting carrier aircraft into the offensive mode, a role for which they had been preparing since the 1930s.

Cunningham's initial plan was to launch the attack on October 21, Trafalgar Day in British naval history, but a shipboard fire scotched the effort, forcing the strike to be rescheduled. The new date, November 11, was also a notable anniversary: it marked the armistice to end World War I. When the old carrier *Eagle* had to drop out, the new *Illustrious* took center stage, but she could muster only twenty-one strike aircraft against Taranto. These were relatively new, though old-looking, Fairey Swordfish biplanes. *Swordfish Attack at Taranto* depicts the events of the 11th as the carrier's first dozen Swordfish swooped down on the slumbering Italian fleet and unloaded flares and torpedoes. A second wave of nine aircraft came later, compounding the damage. The British sank the battleship *Cavour*, which never returned to service, and put two others, the *Littorio* and the *Duilio*, out of action until the following spring. The British pilots and their flimsy "Stringbags," as the biplanes were called, had knocked out the Italian battleship threat and ushered in a new era in naval warfare.

Launch Against the Bismarck
British Royal Navy

Robert Taylor

IN THE SPRING OF 1941, THE GERMAN NAVY WAS POISED TO MOUNT AN OFFENSIVE IN the Atlantic. Under the plan, a number of heavy-gun surface ships would attack Allied merchant shipping, just as the cruiser *Admiral Graf Spee* had done at the outset of war in the autumn of 1939. For various reasons, not all the ships were able to join the contingent, so the task force that set out in mid-May was limited to the battleship *Bismarck* and the heavy cruiser *Prinz Eugen*. The *Bismarck*, armed with eight 15-inch (38cm) guns, was a truly formidable warship, and the breakout by the two ships sent shudders through the British. The sense of unease was heightened considerably when capital ships of the Royal Navy challenged the Germans on May 24, 1941. The *Bismarck*'s gunnery sank the battle cruiser *Hood*, the embodiment of British national pride, and damaged the new battleship *Prince of Wales*. British gunfire inflicted only minor damage on the *Bismarck*.

The German task force commander, Rear Admiral Gunther Lutjens, detached the *Prinz Eugen* and proceeded on alone in the *Bismarck*. The battleship headed for a safe haven in Nazi-occupied France. On May 25, the British aircraft carrier *Victorious* launched a strike of Swordfish torpedo planes against the German ship. These were planes of the same type used in the attack on Taranto six months earlier, but they did not enjoy similar success. They failed to strike the German ship, and the *Bismarck*'s gunnery did not hit them—it was a draw. On May 26, it was the turn of Force H, a British task force dispatched from the Mediterranean, to go after the *Bismarck*. The task force was built around the carrier *Ark Royal*, the battle cruiser *Renown*, and the light cruiser *Sheffield*. As the *Victorious* had done a day earlier, the *Ark Royal*, sent off a flight of Swordfish in an attempt to cripple the German behemoth. *Launch Against the Bismarck* vividly depicts the tough launch, with wind speeds of fifty miles per hour (80kph), a violently pitching flight deck, and a wild green sea.

Sink the Bismarck

British Royal Navy

Stan Stokes

WHEN THE *ARK ROYAL* LAUNCHED HER COVEY OF FIFTEEN TORPEDO-ARMED SWORDFISH, she was about fifty miles (80km) away from her massive target, the *Bismarck*. Unfortunately, several Swordfish attacked the British cruiser *Sheffield* by mistake; by a stroke of good luck, however, all of them missed. Yet the failed strike did serve a useful purpose: it demonstrated the ineffectiveness of the torpedoes' magnetic exploders. For the second attack, the torpedoes were set to explode on contact with the hull of an enemy ship. The second strike went off at about seven o'clock on the evening of May 26, 1941, when the *Bismarck* was thirty-eight miles (61km) away. The strike force leader was Lieutenant Commander Tim Coode. Each of the fifteen biplanes had a crew of three—a pilot, an observer, and an air gunner.

As they neared the target, the British planes split up into subgroups to attack from different directions, making it more difficult for the Germans to mount an effective defense. The Swordfish had to come in low, slow, and straight—traveling slower than 100 knots and maintaining an altitude below 100 feet (30m). On board the German battleship was a gunnery officer named Baron Burkard von Mullenheim-Rechberg. Ludovic Kennedy's fine book *Pursuit* quotes the German officer's reaction to the first Swordfish attack: "It was incredible to see such obsolete-looking planes have the nerve to attack a fire-spitting mountain like *Bismarck*." And now here came still more of them.

The German ship sent up a wall of antiaircraft bullets. To the oncoming pilots the tracers looked like multicolored billiard balls: red, green, orange, and white. Two planes made hits, one amidships that did no damage and one on the giant battleship's rudder. This proved to be a fatal wound: it jammed the rudder fifteen degrees to port. The crippled *Bismarck* could now only steam in circles, unable to bear a straight course to France. The men aboard the great dreadnought were doomed. On the morning of May 27, the British battleships *King George V* and *Rodney* approached the *Bismarck* and pounded her with their big guns, damaging her irreparably. The German crew scuttled their ship, many following it to the bottom. Few of the sailors aboard the *Bismarck* survived.

USS Enterprise

United States Navy

Thomas Skinner

AS THE HOUR GROWS LATE, CREW MEMBERS HURRY TO GET BACK ABOARD THEIR SHIP before liberty expires. Their memories of shore leave will have to sustain them for many months of hard work at sea to come. In that time, the *Enterprise* will take her place as the U.S. warship that did the most to bring about victory in the Pacific during World War II. The ship accumulated twenty battle stars during the protracted conflict.

The *Enterprise* was part of the Hawaiian Detachment established at Pearl Harbor in the autumn of 1939. In November 1941, as part of a task force commanded by Vice Admiral William Halsey, she set out from Pearl to deliver Marine fighter planes to Wake Island. Rough seas kept her from reaching her homeport before the fateful Japanese air raid. Had she been damaged or destroyed on December 7, as were so many others, history would have been dramatically different. As it was, she participated in hit-and-run raids in early 1942, accompanied the *Hornet* on the Doolittle raid in April, and made a key contribution to the defeat of the Japanese at Midway in June. That autumn she was damaged at Guadalcanal and, after the loss of the *Wasp* and the *Hornet*, was the lone operational U.S. carrier in the South Pacific. As the Central Pacific amphibious campaign unfolded, she took part in one action after another, including the great battles near the Marianas and the Philippines. Toward war's end, the *Enterprise* specialized in night operations. On Navy Day 1945, she was moored in the Hudson River off New York to be honored for her heroic service by President Harry Truman.

The carrier's story was superbly told in *The Big E*, written in the early 1960s by Commander Ed Stafford, a naval aviator who had demonstrated his knowledge of American literature on the TV quiz show *The $64,000 Question*. Drawing on a flair for words and extensive aviation experience, he fashioned a fitting literary testament to the achievements of the *Enterprise* and her men. More recently, Dr. Steve Ewing has worked with the crew to establish memorials to the great ship at Patriots Point in Charleston, South Carolina; at the naval museum in Bremerton, Washington; and at the National Museum of Naval Aviation in Pensacola, Florida.

Soryu Steams

Imperial Japanese Navy

Tom Freeman

Lieutenant Commander Minoru Genda, an experienced carrier pilot, was the talented strategist behind the surprise attack on Pearl Harbor.

MUCH ADVANCE THOUGHT AND PREPARATION UNDERGIRDED THE IMPERIAL JAPANESE Navy's raid on Pearl Harbor in December 1941. Having gathered intelligence on the American fleet's pattern of operations in and around Hawaii, Japanese naval commanders had decided to attack on a Sunday morning, when American alertness would be at its lowest. The plan was to catch the U.S. warships by surprise so the Japanese could knock them out in a single blow, and thus prevent them from interfering with the Imperial Navy's planned offensive operations into Southeast Asia. In anticipation of the surprise attack, the Japanese also converted armor-piercing battleship projectiles into bombs that could be dropped from nearly two miles (3km) above the harbor, and could penetrate into the vital workings of the American ships. The Japanese made sure to demolish U.S. airfields on the island of Oahu at the outset in order to eliminate or minimize the Americans' ability to launch fighter planes that could interfere with the raid. And the Japanese came with six aircraft carriers so they could send more than 300 airplanes—fighters, torpedo planes, and bombers— against Hawaii and thus apply overwhelming force. Much of this carefully crafted strategy sprang from the fertile mind of Lieutenant Commander Minoru Genda, a brilliant naval aviator who not only conceived many elements of the plan but also worked to rehearse those who would execute it when the time came.

As Professor Paul Dull described in his *Battle History of the Imperial Japanese Navy, 1941–1945*, the ships of the planned attack force began gathering in late November in the Tankan Bay (also called Hitokappu Bay) on the island of Etorofu in the remote Kurile island chain in the North Pacific. The carriers put out fake message traffic to deceive Americans into believing they were operating elsewhere. Finally, it was time to take yet another step in the Japanese effort to become a major regional power. On the morning of November 26, 1941, the twenty-eight ships of the force weighed anchor and moved into formation for the long, lonely journey across the Pacific to Hawaii. In this painting, a Japanese Navy flying boat patrols in the background and a tugboat is alongside as the carrier *Soryu* heads out of the bay and into the open seas beyond.

Akagi

Imperial Japanese Navy

Tom Freeman

THE JAPANESE FLAG OFFICER IN CHARGE OF THE HAWAII OPERATION WAS VICE ADMIRAL Chuichi Nagumo, an experienced officer with extensive knowledge of torpedoes, but less enthusiasm for naval aviation. He had become more cautious as he grew older and would have preferred to lead Japanese expeditions to the south, rather than the riskier one to Pearl Harbor. His flagship was the *Akagi*. Like the American *Lexington* and *Saratoga*, the *Akagi* was a product of the Washington Treaty of 1922. Originally built as a battle cruiser, she was converted to an aircraft carrier under the terms of the treaty.

As Tom Freeman's painting *Akagi* reveals, the weather during the long trek toward Hawaii was not pleasant. To prevent the attack force from being spotted and reported—which would have eliminated the advantage of surprise—a route north of the standard shipping lanes was chosen. The ships of the task force also observed strict radio silence as another means of avoiding detection. If the ships were seen, the plan was to reverse course and return to Japan. While heading eastward, the force encountered heavy seas, fog, and winter gale-force winds. The weather made sea-keeping difficult, but helped shroud the ships from outside eyes.

On December 1, the powers in Japan made the decision that the raid would go forward, and Vice Admiral Nagumo received the appropriate orders the following day. As the force steamed to its launching point some 230 miles (370km) north of Hawaii, the wind and seas calmed, allowing for underway fueling. The force was also able to increase speed to meet the planned timetable.

Commander Fuchida Takes Off

Imperial Japanese Navy

Tom Freeman

IN SEPTEMBER 1941, LIEUTENANT COMMANDER MITSUO FUCHIDA, A VETERAN NAVAL aviator, reported to the carrier *Akagi* and became commander of all the air groups in Japan's First Air Fleet. Soon afterward, his friend Commander Minoru Genda informed him of a possible attack on Pearl Harbor. This at first seemed inconceivable to Fuchida, but his pilots soon began a time of strenuous practice, mostly involving the dropping of aerial torpedoes, though they were not told about the prospective target. During the journey to Oahu, excitement ran high through the Japanese flagship. As she approached the launch point, the *Akagi* raised the signal flag for the letter Z, which had been used by Admiral Heihachiro Togo on his flagship during the victorious Battle of Tsushima Strait in 1905.

At six o'clock on the morning of December 7, 1941, the launch of the first wave of 183 fighters, torpedo planes, and bombers began. Within fifteen minutes, all the planes of the first group—including that of Commander Fuchida, which was launched from the *Akagi*—roared off the carrier decks and into history. Unlike most carriers, as the painting shows, the *Akagi*'s bridge was on the port side of the ship, an experiment that was not notably successful. As the morning brightened, the planes approached their target. Fuchida was in a rear seat in the group commander's plane so he could devote his full attention to commanding the operation; another pilot sat at the controls. At 7:49 A.M., as the plane approached Oahu, the American fleet was enjoying the last peaceful Sunday it would have for nearly four years. Fuchida directed his radioman to send the Morse code attack signal. Within minutes he sent another message, "Tora, tora, tora," a repetition of the word "tiger" in Japanese, indicating that the Japanese had achieved complete surprise.

Battleship Row
Imperial Japanese Navy

Stan Stokes

THROUGHOUT THE PERIOD BETWEEN THE WORLD WARS, CONVENTIONAL WISDOM HELD that battleships were the ultimate warships. The war plans of both the U.S. and Japanese navies anticipated that the battle lines of both nations would eventually meet up for a gunnery duel on the high seas, somewhere in the western Pacific. The press believed the same thing. British author Hector C. Bywater, the leading naval journalist of his time, published a novel in 1925 titled *The Great Pacific War*. As his biographer, William Honan, observed, Bywater's imaginative plot included a number of prophetic elements. Among them was the scenario in which the Japanese would conduct a surprise attack against the U.S. Navy while the two countries were still negotiating to preserve the peace.

In recognition of the importance of the battleship, President Franklin D. Roosevelt had decreed in the spring of 1940 that the U.S. Battle Force should remain in Hawaii following that year's fleet war game, rather than returning to its customary base in southern California. His intention was to deter Japanese advances in the Far East; instead, he made the battleships an inviting target for carrier-based Japanese bombers and torpedo planes.

Battleship Row captures the moment as a B5N2 Kate attack bomber drops its weapon. Soon after, the port side of the *West Virginia* would be pummeled by that torpedo and seven others unloaded by still more Kates. The *Tennessee*, which can be glimpsed behind the *West Virginia*, suffered relatively minor damage.

Lieutenant Claude Ricketts, onboard the *West Virginia*, ordered that water be flooded into tanks on the ship's starboard side so she would sink on an even keel. The Japanese succeeded in their immediate objective: to knock out the battleships as part of a plan to conclude the war within a few months. The *West Virginia* was so severely damaged that she was unable to fight for nearly two years. But it turned out to be a longer war than the Japanese expected; in September 1945, the repaired *West Virginia* was present in Tokyo Bay when Japan surrendered.

Japanese pilots and crew members of B5N2 Kate attack bombers pose on board their carrier, *Kaga*, the day before the attack on Pearl Harbor.

Air Raid, Pearl Harbor

Imperial Japanese Navy

R.G. Smith

IN 1937, LIEUTENANT COMMANDER LOGAN C. RAMSEY, A NAVAL AVIATOR, ENTERED a manuscript in the U.S. Naval Institute's annual General Prize Essay Contest, which was designed to stimulate thinking and writing on naval topics. *Proceedings* magazine published his article under the title "Aerial Attacks on Fleets at Anchor." While the article did not deal with any specific location, it spelled out many of the issues related to an attack on warships in a port or an anchorage. Interestingly, one of the illustrations used with the piece showed U.S. warships at anchor at Lahaina Roads, off the Hawaiian Island of Maui.

Ramsey's suggested remedy for dealing with attacks on immobilized ships was a "dynamic defense": namely, early detection that would lead to a counter-attack before enemy planes could get within range of their target. Although the article was intended to alert fellow Navy officers, it was eerily prescient in many respects, accurately describing a number of elements of the coming Japanese attack. On December 7, 1941, fate assigned Ramsey as the duty officer for Patrol Wing Two at Pearl Harbor. After he saw a Japanese bomb explode on Ford Island, he made his way to a radio room and ordered a plain-language broadcast on all frequencies: "Air raid, Pearl Harbor. This is no drill."

The only U.S. battleship that got under way during the deadly strike was the USS *Nevada*. Already heavily damaged, she is shown here under attack by a Val dive-bomber, readily identifiable by its fixed, rather than retractable, landing gear. The *Nevada*'s officer of the deck at the outset of the air raid was Ensign Joe Taussig. An enemy shot ripped into his leg and twisted it so grotesquely that his foot wound up under his armpit. The leg later had to be amputated. Years later, though, Taussig wrote he would not have changed the outcome. If the U.S. ships had been warned and gone to sea, their antiaircraft defenses were so feeble that he was sure they would have been sunk in deep water with far heavier loss of life than actually occurred.

The Magnificent Fight:
The Battle for Wake Island

United States Marine Corps

John D. Shaw

IN THE 1930S, PAN AMERICAN AIRWAYS PIONEERED TRANSOCEANIC AIR TRAVEL WITH a series of flying boats known as Clippers. In the process, the airline developed air bases on Pacific islands to serve as stepping-stones to Asia. As war approached, the Navy commandeered some of Pan Am's island bases, and sent Marines to defend them. One such island base was at Wake.

In late 1941, Admiral Husband Kimmel, commander in chief of the U.S. Pacific Fleet, dispatched two aircraft carriers to transport fighter planes to outlying islands—the *Lexington* to Midway and the *Enterprise* to Wake. The *Enterprise* carried twelve F4F-3 Wildcats of Marine Fighting Squadron 211, commanded by Major Paul Putnam. The squadron reached Wake on the morning of December 4. The pilots were new to their planes, and they had precious little help when it came to flying or maintaining them.

Disaster struck on December 8 as Japanese Nell bombers hit the island, mauling the island's support facilities and putting eight of the twelve fighter planes out of commission. Another bombing attack followed on December 10. Captain Henry T. Elrod attacked the bombers and shot down one; his bullets and those of antiaircraft guns damaged three more. The next day the Japanese tried to invade Wake, but the shore batteries and marine aviators drove away their ships. Shown here are Captain Elrod and his crew preparing to take off in squadron plane number eleven, which bombed the destroyer *Kisaragi*; she later exploded and sank. Elrod landed his plane, but it was so badly damaged it could serve only to supply parts for others.

On December 23, the Japanese invaded Wake in force, overwhelmed the defenders, and captured the island. By this time, Captain Elrod had become a Marine infantryman, and stood between his men and the invaders. Just before dawn a Japanese soldier, who had pretended to be dead, shot and killed Elrod. For his efforts in the defense of Wake, Elrod became the first Marine aviator of the war to earn a Medal of Honor.

Butch O'Hare Meets the 1st Chutai

United States Navy

Hugh Polder

Lieutenant Butch O'Hare and his squadron skipper, Lieutenant Commander Jimmy Thach, pose in front of an F4F-3 Wildcat.

EDWARD "BUTCH" O'HARE OF ST. LOUIS GOT HIS COMMISSION FROM THE NAVAL Academy in 1937 and performed the obligatory shipboard duty before going into flight training. After winning his aviator's wings at Pensacola, Florida, in May 1940 he reported to Fighting Squadron Three (VF-3), commanded by Lieutenant Jimmy Thach. The squadron skipper and his senior pilots had formed what they called a "humiliation team," which was designed to take cocky young pilots up for some dogfighting to teach them that they still had a thing or two to learn. It served its purpose well—until O'Hare joined the squadron. From the beginning, he demonstrated that he could fly with the big boys. He was a natural. As Thach later explained in his oral history: "Butch O'Hare was a good athlete. He had a sense of timing and relative motion that he may have been born with, but also he had that competitive spirit. When he got into any kind of a fight like this, he didn't want to lose. He really was dedicated to winning."

The first combat test for VF-3 came on February 20, 1942, while flying from the carrier *Lexington*. She was part of a task force headed for an attack on the Japanese stronghold of Rabaul. That day Thach and O'Hare were aloft in their F4F-3 Wildcats as part of the combat air patrol for the task force. The radio silence that had been observed religiously was suddenly broken with a message from the carrier reporting an incoming snooper. Thach motioned O'Hare to stay and guard the ship while he and his wingman left to shoot down the patrol plane, the first enemy aircraft any in the squadron had seen. O'Hare stayed, but he was anxious to get into action.

His opportunity came that afternoon. A formation of eighteen land-based Betty bombers from Rabaul approached the ship. It comprised two groups of nine bombers, and each group had three V-shaped, three-plane sections. (*Chutai* is the Japanese term for a formation of six to nine aircraft.) Thach, who was up on combat air patrol with other members of the squadron, chewed into the first flight of nine. Between the Wildcats' machine guns and the antiaircraft fire from

below, only one of the nine escaped. O'Hare was then launched as part of a flight of six F4F-3s sent to intercept the second formation of Bettys. When the planes were twelve miles (19km) out, O'Hare and his wingman closed in to attack, but the wingman found that his guns wouldn't fire, so he dived away. Left to his own devices, the aggressive O'Hare methodically shot down five bombers in less than five minutes. He aimed his .50-caliber machine guns at the engines of the bombers and hit repeatedly. Thach, who was still in the air at the time, marveled at a sight he never thought he'd witness: three burning Japanese planes drifting toward the sea simultaneously because O'Hare was dispatching them so quickly. The other four planes flew on toward the *Lexington*. Captain Ted Sherman, the carrier's skipper, managed to maneuver the ship so as to avoid the incoming bombs. The *Lexington* remained unscathed, in large part because of O'Hare's exceptional marksmanship.

For his remarkable feat, O'Hare was awarded the Medal of Honor. He missed out on the Battle of Midway in June because he was back in the United States making a publicity tour to sell war bonds, a chore he disliked because it took him away from the cockpit. O'Hare lost his life in November 1943 when his F4F-3 was shot down while engaged in night-fighter experiments during the invasion of the Gilbert Islands. O'Hare International Airport in Chicago is named in honor of this man who in February 1942 became the Navy's first fighter ace of World War II.

The Hornet's Nest
United States Army Air Forces

John D. Shaw

Jimmy Doolittle, following his promotion to lieutenant general later in the war.

AFTER SUFFERING A STEADY STRING OF DEFEATS IN THE EARLY PART OF THE WAR IN THE Pacific, the United States was looking for a way to fight back—partly to inflict some pain on Japan and partly to build morale at home. Together, the Army Air Forces and Navy succeeded. Navy Lieutenant Hank Miller provided training at Eglin Field in Florida so that bomber pilots could learn to take off from a short runway, that is, the deck of an aircraft carrier.

The twin-engine B-25 aircraft were named for Army Brigadier General Billy Mitchell, who in the early 1920s had been almost fanatical in preaching the gospel of air power. He proclaimed that bombers would make warships obsolete. Now, ironically, a warship was to be the means of transporting land-based planes within striking distance of the Japanese homeland.

The leader of the retaliatory force was Lieutenant Colonel Jimmy Doolittle, who had gained considerable fame as a civilian pilot in the years between the world wars. He is shown here on the deck of the *Hornet*, standing in front of a row of tied-down Mitchells. The man in the khaki baseball cap standing with him is Captain Marc Mitscher, commanding officer of the *Hornet*. Two years later, Mitscher would establish himself as the foremost U.S. carrier admiral of the war.

One of the most accurate wartime movies ever produced was *Thirty Seconds Over Tokyo*, based on a book by Captain Ted Lawson, one of the Army pilots who flew on the Doolittle Raid. Another of the pilots was Lieutenant Don Smith. The actor who portrayed Smith in the film was William S. Phillips. The actor's son and namesake, Bill Phillips, contributed some of the paintings that grace this book. Years after the event, Bill Phillips attended a reunion of the Tokyo raiders and had an opportunity to meet Smith's widow and the great Doolittle himself. As Phillips asked Doolittle about the 1942 raid, he said, "I saw the old airman's face light up, his eyes growing distant."

Compass Heading 270°
United States Army Air Forces

Robert Taylor

WHILE THE APRIL 18, 1942, ATTACK ON JAPAN BECAME POPULARLY KNOWN AS THE "Doolittle Raid," the Navy preferred the title "Halsey-Doolittle Raid," since Vice Admiral William F. Halsey was in overall command of the operation.

Sixteen B-25s were loaded aboard the *Hornet* at Alameda, California, on April 1. The task force got under way the following day. Only then did the crew of the carrier learn that the ship was headed toward Tokyo, because security concerning the mission and the target had been extremely tight. En route, Lieutenant Steve Jurika, formerly an assistant naval attaché in Japan, briefed the Army fliers on what to expect when they got over the target areas in Tokyo and other Japanese cities. After the raid was completed, the planes were to fly on to land in China. The original plan was to launch 500 miles (805km) from Tokyo, but the ships were spotted by Japanese picket boats even farther out, so the planes had to take off from about 650 miles (1,046km) away from Japan.

In this painting, Halsey's flagship, the *Enterprise,* can be seen in the background. In the foreground is the *Hornet*, which has already launched Colonel Doolittle's B-25; another bomber is headed down the deck on its takeoff run. Barely visible above the *Hornet*'s deck are two F4F Wildcats of the combat air patrol that protected the U.S. task force as it ventured into waters near Japan. The fighters were supplied by the *Enterprise* because the *Hornet*'s own planes were down in the hangar deck while the B-25s were on board.

Of the eighty Army airmen on the raid, nearly all survived. A few were captured and executed by the Japanese; one crew landed in the Soviet Union, which was now allied against the Axis powers, and was interned. Doolittle received a Medal of Honor and a two-grade promotion to brigadier general. With tongue in cheek, President Roosevelt said the Army bombers had taken off from the mythical kingdom of Shangri-la. The Navy honored that bit of whimsy by naming one of its wartime carriers the USS *Shangri-La*; Mrs. Doolittle christened the new ship. Above all, the raid, which did little military damage, dealt a severe blow to the Japanese ego. Admiral Yamamoto used the attack to bolster his argument to invade and capture an island on the way to Hawaii: Midway.

Scratch One Flat Top

United States Navy

Stan Stokes

THE JAPANESE STRIKE ON PEARL HARBOR DRAMATICALLY ESTABLISHED THE PRIMACY OF AIRCRAFT carriers as attack weapons in naval warfare. No longer would they be subordinate to battleships. As the navies of both powers moved their pieces on the Pacific chessboard, it was inevitable that a battle would develop that pitted carrier against carrier. The strategic motivation was the continuing Japanese expansion plan to conquer southern Asia. Having gobbled up the Dutch East Indies, the Philippines, Hong Kong, and Singapore, Japanese forces now set their sights on invading Port Moresby in southern New Guinea. That would then serve as a stepping-stone to nearby Australia.

But the Americans had plans of their own. Code breakers in Hawaii decrypted Japanese radio messages and divined their intentions. Admiral Chester Nimitz sent a task force built around the carriers *Lexington* and *Yorktown* to intercept and thwart a force that included the light carrier *Shoho* and two Pearl Harbor veterans, the *Shokaku* and the *Zuikaku*. The small carrier, accompanying the

transports, would venture forth, and the two large ones would pounce as the Americans responded. They responded all right, and on May 7, 1942, a strike force of ninety-three planes descended on the hapless *Shoho*. She was pounded with bombs from the Dauntlesses and torpedoes from TBD Devastators.

The TBD, which had entered fleet service in 1937, was the U.S. Navy's first low-wing, all-metal monoplane. But, like the British Swordfish, it had to fly low and slow toward the target to deliver its weapon accurately. Shown here is a Devastator from the *Lexington*'s Torpedo Two flying over the burning *Shoho* after delivering its torpedo. The pilot is Lieutenant R.F. Farrington, and his two enlisted crew members are T.R. Wiebe and Walter N. Nelson.

The first bomb hit in the multiweapon attack was delivered by Lieutenant Commander Robert E. Dixon, skipper of Scouting Two from the "*Lex*." Later, as he flew over the scene and watched bombs and torpedoes rip open the *Shoho* and leave her a burning wreck, he sent a classic voice radio message back to his shipmates: "Scratch one flattop! Dixon to carrier, scratch one flattop!"

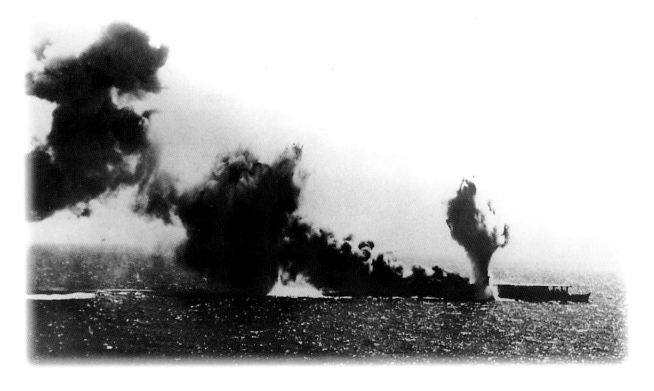

The *Shoho* explodes and burns after absorbing a combination of bombs and torpedoes from American carrier planes. She was the first major Japanese ship sunk in the war. The battle also damaged the carrier *Shokaku* and killed many pilots from the *Zuikaku*, they were not able to take part in the subsequent Battle of Midway.

Lady Lex Is Hit

Imperial Japanese Navy

R.G. Smith

As one of the U.S. Navy's first two large aircraft carriers, the *Lexington* made enormous contributions during her fourteen-plus years of active service, even though her combat career was relatively brief. During the annual fleet problem in early 1929, she was part of the defending force as mock war games centered on the Panama Canal. Her sister, *Saratoga*, one of the attacking ships, demonstrated the practicality of the carrier task force concept—that carriers could play an offensive role in naval warfare and not just serve in a support role for the heavy-gun battleships. Later that year, the *Lex* had an entirely different mission as a result of a power failure in the Pacific Northwest. In the winter of 1929–30, she moored at a pier in Tacoma, Washington, and supplied all of the city's electrical power from her shipboard generators. In 1931 she provided earthquake relief in Managua, Nicaragua.

In February 1932, it was the *Lexington's* turn to demonstrate the striking power of aircraft carriers. On a quiet Sunday morning she unleashed a surprise attack of aircraft toward the island of Oahu, Hawaii. The planes caught the Army defenders flatfooted, and in the mock battle the aircraft from the *Lex* were the clear winners. On another quiet Sunday morning nearly ten years later it was the Japanese Navy that staged a surprise air raid on Oahu, but this time with devastating results. When that war began in December 1941, the *Lexington* was mercifully spared, being away from Pearl Harbor on a mission to deliver Marine Corps aircraft to Midway Island. Later in the month, she was dispatched toward Wake Island as part of a force to relieve the Americans who were at peril of invasion by the Japanese. She was called back because of the threat of Japanese forces nearby, and Wake Island fell.

In February 1942, she was steaming toward Rabaul on New Britain and was saved from destruction or serious damage by Lieutenant (j.g.) Butch O'Hare, as described earlier. In April her air group made a successful surprise attack on Lae and Salamaua on the island of New Guinea, and in May she and the carrier *Yorktown* comprised the centerpiece of Rear Admiral Frank Jack Fletcher's force during the Battle of the Coral Sea, which was important in sparing Australia

from attack and possible invasion. But it was there on May 8 that her luck ran out. Late that morning she absorbed hits from five Japanese torpedoes, launched by the planes shown here. Dive-bombers also made hits, and the ship was soon ablaze and torn by internal explosions. The crew made an orderly evacuation. Because Japanese submarines were in the area, and because the *Lex* was beyond saving, the destroyer *Phelps* was ordered to finish her off with American torpedoes. The fifteen-year-old pioneer descended quickly and disappeared. One misty-eyed veteran delivered her eulogy when he said, "She was a lady to the finish, never showing her skirts."

Onboard ship during the *Lexington's* wartime actions was war correspondent Stanley Johnston of the *Chicago Tribune*. He got to know crew members well and wrote a book about the carrier, *Queen of the Flat-Tops*, ironically titled since the carrier had already been sunk by the time the tribute was published. Even so, for a reading public eager for news in an era before television, the book provided a great deal of information about the flavor of life onboard a carrier and the nature of carrier operations, and gave insights into the men of the crew and the air group. Johnston's presence onboard ship gained him the confidence of his subjects.

After the sinking of the *Lex*, Johnston and other survivors returned to the United States on board the transport *Barnett*. Somehow, perhaps through the *Lexington's* former executive officer, Commander Mort Seligman, Johnston learned about the Japanese plans to capture Midway—information gained from the code breaking of Japanese messages. On June 7, during the latter stages of the Midway battle, the *Tribune* published an article by Johnston. A classic scoop, it revealed that the U.S. Navy knew in advance about the Japanese plans and the makeup of the attacking fleet, but it did not specify intercepted messages as the source of the information. Johnston testified before a grand jury, but the Navy chose not to participate because it did not want to reveal its code breaking successes. As it happened, the Japanese apparently did not connect the article with broken codes, and the government decided not to pursue the matter.

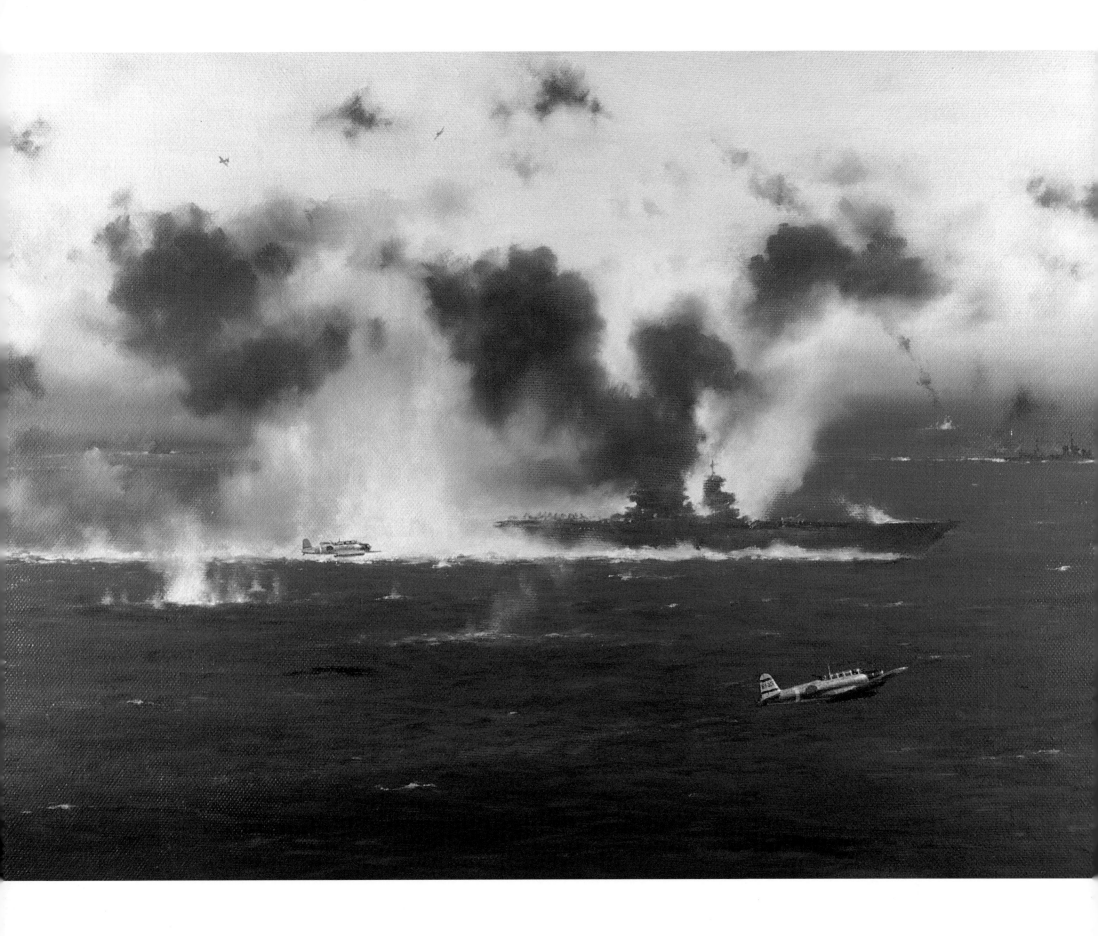

Stung by the Wasp
Royal Air Force

Stan Stokes

David McCampbell, as landing signal officer, stands at the stern end of the *Wasp*'s flight deck and uses paddles to signal an incoming plane about its approach. LSOs played a vital role in carrier operations by coaching aircraft back onto the deck. After the *Wasp* was sunk in September 1942, McCampbell returned to the United States to train others to be LSOs. Not until 1944 did he finally get a flying job in combat.

IN 1942, LIEUTENANT DAVID MCCAMPBELL, WHO LATER BECAME the U.S. Navy's top fighter ace of the war, had a nonflying job as landing signal officer of the *Wasp*. His role was to stand at the stern of the carrier and use paddles to guide pilots as they made their approach to land on deck.

In the Mediterranean that spring, the British-held island of Malta, south of Sicily, faced heavy threat from air attacks. Prime Minister Winston Churchill asked the United States for help, so in April the *Wasp* steamed up the River Clyde to Glasgow, Scotland, where she took aboard a load of forty-seven land-based Spitfire fighter planes. She proceeded to ferry them through the Strait of Gibraltar and launched them to reinforce Malta. The Germans soon learned of their arrival and decimated the Spitfires, many of them on the ground. So Churchill asked again, and in May the *Wasp* carried in another load of Spitfires. With her came the British carrier *Eagle*, which had a smaller batch. They launched their broods on May 9.

One of the British flyers, Sergeant-Pilot Smith, lost his belly tank on takeoff from the *Wasp* and thus did not have enough fuel for the long flight to Malta. Though he'd never landed on a carrier before, had never flown a Spitfire before, and had no tailhook to stop him, Smith elected to return to the carrier rather than ditch. Predictably, he came in high and fast, and McCampbell signaled that his approach was no good. Smith did better the second time, settled down, then used a hand brake to bring the plane to a screeching halt a few feet short of the forward edge of the flight deck. That evening McCampbell and his shipmates, much impressed by the achievement, awarded Smith U.S. naval aviator's wings.

The carrier's action saved Malta. Soon afterward came a message from Churchill: "Many thanks to you all for the timely help. Who said a *Wasp* couldn't sting twice?"

Looking for Nagumo

United States Navy

Craig Kodera

IN JUNE 1942, THE JAPANESE NAVY SENT OUT A TASK FORCE TO INVADE AND OCCUPY Midway Island as a means of gaining territory that much closer to Hawaii and providing a wider defensive perimeter for the Japanese home islands. Another objective was to lure the American carriers into action and wipe them out as a threat. Commander in Chief Isoroku Yamamoto was a shrewd and adventurous gambler, but this time the tables were turned by American code breakers who knew the Japanese were coming.

The job of looking for the approaching enemy fleet fell to PBY Catalina flying boats, a type developed in the late 1930s as a long-range patrol bomber. Shown here is a PBY from Patrol Squadron 44. On the morning of June 3, 1942, the plane and its crew were out in search of the Midway-bound Japanese invasion force under Vice Admiral Chuichi Nagumo, who had earlier commanded the successful raid against Pearl Harbor. The pilot in 44-P-4 that morning was Ensign Jack Reid. He flew 700 miles (1,126km) on his outbound leg and saw nothing but clouds and empty ocean. With another look through the binoculars he spotted the Japanese carrier force. At 9:25 A.M. he flashed a two-word contact report, "Main body." He had seen the twenty-seven ships of the transport group bringing the potential invaders. The vital carriers were still to be spotted, however, and early the next morning that duty fell to PBY pilots Lieutenant Howard Ady and Lieutenant William Chase, who searched to the northwest of Midway. They spotted their prey around 5:30 A.M., and Chase radioed in a message, "Many planes heading Midway. Bearing 320, distance 150."

The report provided a moment of satisfaction for the head of the patrol operation. That was Commander Logan Ramsey, who had been on duty at Pearl six months earlier and sent the dramatic message, "Air raid, Pearl Harbor. This is no drill." Walter Lord's masterful book on Midway, *Incredible Victory*, records Ramsey's comments during the tense time before the battle as he waited at Midway while others were out doing the flying: "I feel like a June bride. I know it's going to happen, but I don't know what it will be like."

Dauntless Against the Rising Sun

United States Navy

William S. Phillips

For many years—until it standardized with the Air Force in 1962—the Navy used a distinctive system for designating its aircraft. The first letter or letters indicated the aircraft's function, and the last letter specified the manufacturer. A number could also be inserted to indicate a later aircraft of the same type and manufacturer. A number after the hyphen indicated an upgrade. The Dauntless, the workhorse Navy attack plane during the first half of the war in the Pacific, bore the letters SBD—a scout-bomber built by Douglas. As author-pilot Barrett Tillman reported in his book *The Dauntless Dive Bomber of World War II*, the first SBD-1s entered squadron service with the Marine Corps in June 1940. The Navy received the first SBD-2s in November of that year. These models had more fuel capacity, more armor plate, increased gun armament, and bulletproof windshields. *Dauntless Against the Rising Sun* depicts SBD-3s, which entered the fleet in March 1941. They had all the SBD-2 modifications but on a lighter airframe.

The versatility of the Dauntless is demonstrated by these planes of Scouting Five, a *Yorktown* squadron commanded by Lieutenant Wallace Short. During the Battle of the Coral Sea in June, 1942, the squadron had been Bombing Five. Now, just a month later, with the addition of replacement Dauntlesses from different sources, it was redesignated VS-5 rather than VB-5. On the morning of June 4, the *Yorktown* intercepted radio reports of the PBY sighting of the Japanese carriers to the northwest of Midway. At dawn that day, VS-5 sent aloft ten SBDs on scouting missions to search for still more enemy aircraft carriers. Following standard procedure for scouting, the Dauntlesses operated in two plane sections, as shown here, and were armed with 500-pound (227kg) bombs for possible use against enemy ships. But the real mission was to locate the enemy so that other SBDs could come in with their 1,000-pounders (454kg) and deliver a heavier punch. SBDs from VS-5 and other squadrons from both the *Yorktown* and the *Enterprise* did just that. Dauntlesses from those two carriers accomplished the heavy destruction in the tide-turning Battle of Midway.

They Gave Their All

United States Navy

William S. Phillips

As torpedo squadrons from the three American carriers prepared to attack the Japanese approaching Midway, they hoped to duplicate their success from the Battle of the Coral Sea. The commanding officer of the *Hornet*'s Torpedo Squadron Eight was Lieutenant Commander John Waldron, who had been an officer since graduating from the Naval Academy in 1924. He had trained his pilots with an intensity that approached fanaticism, but he had as yet no combat experience, nor did the men in his flock. Because of the Halsey-Doolittle raid in April 1942, the *Hornet* had not been able to reach the Coral Sea in time to take part in that battle.

On June 3, 1942, the night before the Midway confrontation, Waldron delivered a message to his aviators that included these words: "My greatest hope is that we encounter a favorable tactical situation, but if we don't, and worst comes to worst, I want each of us to do his utmost to destroy our enemies. If there is only one plane left to make a final run in, I want that man to go in and get a hit." His words proved sadly prophetic. The plan was for the *Hornet*'s air group to stage a coordinated attack on the Japanese carriers, but this never happened. Waldron led his squadron toward the enemy formation, but the fighters and dive-bombers from his carrier were not with him. At 9:20 in the morning, having sighted the Japanese carriers, the skipper signaled to his inexperienced charges and began the maddeningly slow run-in from nine miles (14km) out.

Down from above roared the Japanese Zeros, fast and maneuverable planes that poured bullet after bullet into the hapless Devastators. In the rear seats, enlisted gunners attempted to shoot down the enemy fighters but were greatly overmatched. One after another, the TBDs were hit, caught fire, and fell into the sea. Waldron's plane soon received the same treatment. Others saw him stand up briefly in his flaming cockpit, but his war was over even before he could deliver his torpedo. Finally, only Ensign George Gay was left. Though wounded, he was able to get in close enough to drop his torpedo, which missed. He then flew over the enemy carrier and tried to turn and run. That's when the Zeros

ABOVE: Ensign George Gay (front row, center), poses with Torpedo Squadron Eight. Ensign Gay was the only member of the squadron to survive the devastating raid on Japanese carriers at Midway.
LEFT: Lieutenant Commander John Waldron in front of one of Torpedo Squadron Eight's Douglas TBD-1 Devastators.

got him as well, and his plane plunged into the Pacific. He managed to hide under a seat cushion from the TBD as the battle swirled on around him. An American destroyer later rescued him. Of the fifteen planes and thirty men of VT-8 that went after the Japanese that morning, George Gay was, as in the title of his memoir, the *Sole Survivor*.

Midway–The Fifth Minute
United States Navy

R.G. Smith

FOR VARIOUS REASONS, THE STRIKE GROUPS FROM THE THREE U.S. CARRIERS AT MIDWAY were not able to mount coordinated attacks on the morning of June 4, 1942. The *Hornet's* torpedo planes found the Japanese, but the Japanese chewed them up. Fliers from the other two carriers, *Yorktown* and *Enterprise,* went out in search of the Japanese striking force but initially had trouble locating them. Commander Wade McClusky was in charge of the *Enterprise* air group. After flying for a while and seeing only empty ocean, he spotted the Japanese destroyer *Arashi* hightailing it to the northeast. She had left the carriers' protective screen to drop a depth charge on the submarine *Nautilus.* Now she was returning to the carrier formation and unwittingly pointing McClusky and the SBD dive-bombers toward their target.

Once overhead, McClusky pushed over into a dive on an enemy carrier. Squadrons from both the *Enterprise* and the *Yorktown* followed suit. Their assaults were unhindered by Japanese fighters because many of the Zeros had been drawn away to defend against the attacks by the American torpedo planes. Lieutenant Commander Jimmy Thach, assisting the torpedo planes in his Wildcat fighter, was busily engaged in dealing with the defending Zeros. As he later explained, "I saw this glint in the sun, and it just looked like a beautiful silver waterfall, these dive-bombers coming down." Beginning at 10:24 A.M., the SBDs scored hit after hit on the Japanese carriers. The effect of their bombing was magnified because the Japanese planes on deck were in the process of being refueled and rearmed, so their bombs were exposed and unprotected.

Within five minutes, as shown here, three Japanese carriers, the *Kaga,* the *Akagi,* and the *Soryu* were ablaze and smoking. The *Hiryu* was still intact and managed to launch a strike that crippled the *Yorktown,* but the *Hiryu* was doomed as well. Meanwhile, Thach had been shooting down enemy fighters. Afterward, flying back toward the *Yorktown,* he felt a slippery liquid on his leg and feared it was blood. Finally, reluctantly, he rubbed his glove against it and brought it up to his eyes. As he later remembered, "I was never so glad to see oil on my hands in my life."

Ensign George Gay (left) and Lieutenant E. Scott McCuskey (in cockpit). McCuskey, an early Navy fighter ace, shot down five enemy planes at the Battle of Midway.

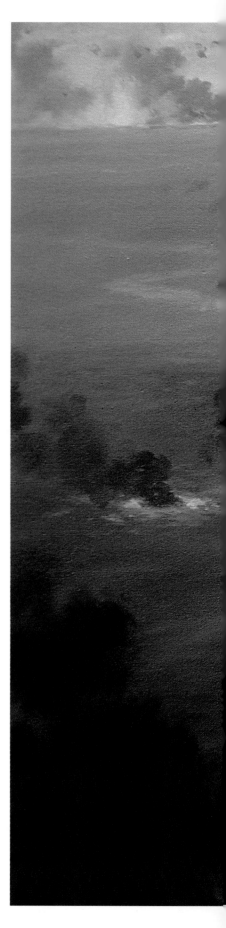

Best on Deck

United States Navy

James Dietz

IN 1932 RICHARD H. BEST GRADUATED FROM THE NAVAL ACADEMY, WHICH WAS BY FAR the primary commissioning source between the world wars. After serving the obligatory initial period on a surface ship, he proceeded to flight training and won his wings. By June of 1942, after working his way up the promotion ladder, he was a lieutenant in command of Bombing Squadron Six on the *Enterprise*.

As Walter Lord describes in his book *Incredible Victory*, Dick Best was worried when he learned from Rear Admiral Raymond Spruance about the plan to intercept the Japanese invasion force. Best's wife and young child were in Honolulu. If American intelligence was wrong, perhaps the enemy was headed for Hawaii rather than Midway. On the morning of June 4, Best took off as part of the *Enterprise* strike group. Both of the ship's SBD squadrons arrived over the Japanese carriers almost simultaneously. Best pushed over into a near-vertical dive and put a bomb on the flight deck of a carrier, probably the *Akagi*, Admiral Nagumo's flagship. Bombs from his squadron mates fell on the after end of the flight deck and wreaked havoc on the planes there.

Best returned to the *Enterprise* to report that one Japanese carrier was still unscathed. *Best on Deck* captures the scene as, late that afternoon, he flew off again. One yellow-shirted member of the deck crew holds up a blackboard displaying the latest information, while another prepares to drop a flag and send him on his way. Best and other American bombers converged over the *Hiryu* that afternoon and administered a pounding that inflicted fatal wounds. She sank the following day.

Meanwhile, Best guided his Dauntless back to the "Big E" and completed what proved to be his last carrier flight ever. The worn-out Best was coughing up blood, and doctors said that a faulty oxygen bottle had activated latent tuberculosis. He went ashore, and early in 1944 was retired from the Navy because of physical disability. Best recovered from TB and went on to a second career in the private sector. In October 2001, the tall, thin Best died at age ninety-one. The man who had been retired because of ill health had outlived all the other squadron commanding officers from the Battle of Midway.

Only One Survived

United States Navy

Craig Kodera

GRUMMAN TURNED OUT THE FIRST PRODUCTION MODELS OF THE TBF-1 TORPEDO bomber in January 1942. In March of that year a group of pilots and air crew members from Torpedo Squadron Eight was detached and sent to the Grumman factory on Long Island to pick up the initial delivery of six airplanes. The planes were able to drop new torpedoes from a higher altitude and at higher speeds than the TBDs. Meanwhile, the main portion of the squadron, still flying TBDs, was deployed to the Pacific on board the carrier *Hornet*. The TBF crews took their new planes to the West Coast and Pearl Harbor, and on June 1 arrived at Midway Island, where they learned that a major operation was in the works.

Early on the morning of June 4, the six torpedo planes took off from Midway to seek out and attack the Japanese carrier force. It was to be the combat debut for the TBF. The first of the new aircraft delivered to the squadron had been painted with the side number 8-T-1, which indicated the squadron number, function, and plane number. Its pilot was Ensign Albert Earnest, and he had two crewmen. Aviation Machinist's Mate J.D. Manning was assigned to the .50-caliber turret gun atop the plane and Aviation Radioman Harry Ferrier operated the tunnel gun at the bottom.

A pack of Japanese Zeros set upon the newcomers and began picking them off with their machine guns. After the Zeros had finished a second gunnery run, Ferrier looked over his shoulder and saw that Manning had stopped firing. As he later wrote, "The sight of his lifeless body startled me. Quite suddenly, I was a scared, mature old man at 18." Both Earnest and Ferrier were wounded on subsequent passes by the Zeros, which greatly outnumbered them. Earnest launched his torpedo toward the Japanese but did no damage. At least his plane was still flying; all the other five TBFs were shot down and lost during the mission. Earnest took a wide detour around the Japanese fleet and brought his damaged aircraft back to Midway. That same morning the other members of VT-8 were wiped out in their TBDs. Subsequently, the Navy's TBFs were named Avengers as a tribute to the lost members of Torpedo Squadron Eight, and to indicate the planes' new purpose.

Dauntless (SBD)

United States Navy

Ted Wilbur

THE MAN WHO CREATED THE SBD, ED HEINEMANN, WAS PERHAPS THE MOST CAPABLE and prolific designer in the history of U.S. Navy aircraft. (Among his other notable successes was the A-4 Skyhawk jet bomber of the 1950s.) In the mid-1930s, as the chief engineer for Northrop, he designed the XBT-1 dive-bomber. In 1937, as Barrett Tillman describes in *The Dauntless Dive Bomber of World War II*, the Douglas Aircraft Company took over the Navy contract from Northrop. Now at Douglas, Heinemann continued to refine his previous aircraft. Among his changes was the perforation of the split dive brakes at the after edges of the wings. These holes permitted the plane to dive at a steeper angle than its predecessor, and the new design made for a steadier bombing platform as it dove on its target. The improved version was called the XBT-2. Because it was now a Douglas plane rather than a Northrop model, it was redesignated as XSBD-1, and later the X,

which stood for "experimental," was dropped. In 1939 the Navy's Bureau of Aeronautics began ordering SBDs, and the Dauntless went into production.

Until it was phased out of carrier squadrons in mid-1944, the Dauntless did much to live up to its nickname. The Pacific War featured five battles that pitted carriers against carriers: Coral Sea in May 1942, Midway in June 1942, the Eastern Solomons in August 1942, the Santa Cruz Islands in October 1942, and the Philippine Sea in June 1944. The SBD was the only aircraft type to participate in all of them. Among its biggest fans was Lieutenant Commander James D. "Jig Dog" Ramage, skipper of Bombing Squadron 10 during the battle off the Marianas in the Philippine Sea in 1944. He argued for the SBD's retention, even as the SB2C Helldiver was coming in to take its place. The Dauntlesses assumed training commands in the States at that point, but their place in history was already secure.

Dauntless Gunner

United States Navy

Ted Wilbur

OF THE HUNDREDS OF ENLISTED MEN WHO SERVED ON BOARD EACH AIRCRAFT CARRIER in World War II, only a relative handful got to fly on a regular basis. These were the aviation radio operators and aviation machinist's mates who sat in the rear seats of the attack aircraft: SBDs, TBDs, TBFs, and SB2Cs. These planes had relatively limited self-defense capabilities, partly because they carried fewer forward-firing machine guns than fighters, and also because they were less maneuverable. The remedy was to provide sailors as rear-seat men to operate machine guns and radios. In *Dauntless Gunner*, a sailor on the deck of a carrier hands up a mount that carries two .30-caliber machine guns. Like the pilot with whom he rides, the radioman-gunner is outfitted in flight helmet, goggles, parachute pack, and a yellow Mae West life jacket. The life jacket came by its colorful name because, when inflated, it supposedly resembled the figure of the buxom movie actress of that era.

For the rear-seat men who got the privilege of flying, there was an obvious drawback as well—they shared the fate of the pilots up front, but were powerless to control their own destiny. One truly unfortunate case involved the crew of an SBD from the *Enterprise* during the Battle of Midway. Robert Barde related the story in a Ph.D. dissertation for the University of Maryland. Late in the afternoon of June 4, 1942, he wrote, the Japanese cruiser *Nagara* spotted a life raft bearing the pilot and gunner from a Dauntless. The men were unhurt except for superficial abrasions. Over the next few days an English-speaking officer in the crew of the *Nagara* interrogated the pair and elicited considerable information concerning the American defenses on Midway Island, though apparently little about the American carrier forces. The Japanese took souvenirs from the captives, including the pilot's cigarette lighter, which bore an inscription: "To my matchless husband." As the ship steamed away, the cruiser's captain decided to dispose of the prisoners; they were bound, blindfolded, and thrown overboard.

Unsung

United States Navy

James Dietz

MAINTENANCE CREWS TRULY ARE THE UNSUNG HEROES OF AERIAL COMBAT. Understandably, the pilots of carrier planes received the lion's share of credit for their successes in combat. But they would not have been able to fly their planes or maneuver them effectively without the help of sailors such as the ones pictured here. Mechanics played a vital role in keeping planes running, repairing battle damage, and ensuring that the equipment was in working order.

Artist James Dietz has created this image with a loving eye for detail. The scene is the hangar deck of an American carrier early in the war. Under the left wing of the SBD Dauntless is the star-and-circle insignia that identified it as a U.S. plane. The red ball in the center disappeared soon after the war began to avoid confusion with the red rising-sun insignia on Japanese planes. In the upper right-hand corner of the picture one can see a row of spare propellers, hanging at the ready until needed. Indeed, a carrier was partly a floating warehouse that performed many of the functions of an air station ashore. Perched on a ladder, wrench in hand, cigarettes rolled up in his sleeve, is a sailor wearing the cap of the New York Yankees. Since 1927, the "Bronx Bombers" had been the number one team in baseball, but now a new leader was emerging. The St. Louis Cardinals beat the Yankees in the 1942 World Series and continued to dominate the sport for the remainder of the war.

The man with the screwdriver, up near the cockpit, has a Baby Ruth candy bar peeking out of the pocket of his dungarees. Candy, ice cream, and soft drinks came from a shipboard refreshment stand known as a "gedunk." Like the cigarettes sold for a few pennies a pack in the ship's store, these treats came as a welcome diversion amid the demands of war. Stretched taut near the cockpit is a wire antenna to facilitate communication between the ship and other planes. The mechanic at left rests his foot on one of the landing gear wheels, which will fold up into a pocket on the underside of the wing during flight. Finally, peering around the toolbox in the foreground is a cat. In the early years of the twentieth century, pets were a staple of Navy life onboard ship—yet another reminder of the simple pleasures back home.

Navy Fighter Pilot A.C. "Silver" Emerson

United States Navy

Tom Lea

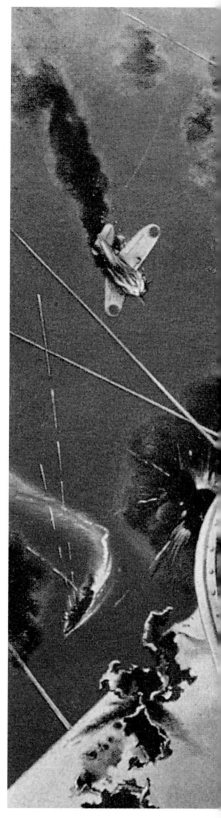

WHILE ONBOARD THE *HORNET* IN 1942, ARTIST TOM LEA WAS IMPRESSED BY LIEUTENANT Alberto C. Emerson, who was nicknamed "Silver" because he was prematurely gray. Earlier in the year, Emerson had been a successful hangar deck officer on the *Yorktown*. Now, as an F4F Wildcat pilot, he was executive officer of VF-72, the carrier's fighter squadron. In part, it was probably this aviator's intensity that attracted the artist's attention.

In the mid-1990s, when he was eighty-seven, Lea recalled his wartime experiences as he talked with Brendan Greeley of *Naval History* magazine. Lea spent quite a bit of time during World War II with Marine Corps units. As he told Greeley, "I think all of us grew personally to hate Japs, and I don't think any Marine I met hated them any worse than Silver Emerson did. He'd come back with his tongue all bloody from biting it in flight." The artist captured Emerson's teeth-gritting intensity—along with the ferocity of aerial combat—in this painting. Only occasionally did Emerson lament the personal aspect involved in killing. After he had set one Japanese bomber afire and watched it fall, he explained to Lea how he saw two crew members climb out onto a wing. "They did look kind of pitiful there, not being able to decide whether to drown or burn to death," Emerson confessed. A few seconds later, the plane exploded.

A fellow member of VF-72, Claude R. Phillips, Jr., was struck by both Emerson's personal charisma and his skill as an aviator, noting that he was "surely the most competent pilot in our squadron. He was an aviator's aviator, a pilot who could make an airplane do almost anything." After surviving the loss of the *Hornet* in October 1942, members of the squadron began operating from the island of Guadalcanal in early February 1943. On the twelfth day of that month, Emerson led a strike against Japanese positions on New Georgia in the central Solomon Islands. Emerson was lost on that mission. Other members of the strike group concluded that he must have been shot down by antiaircraft fire, because he was too capable a fighter pilot to be caught from behind. Reflecting on those wartime years, including the death of Emerson and so many others, has often made Phillips wonder " . . . why it all had to be so."

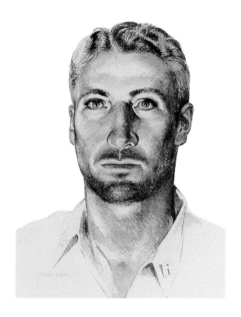

Lieutenant Alberto C. "Silver" Emerson, in a portrait sketch by artist Tom Lea.

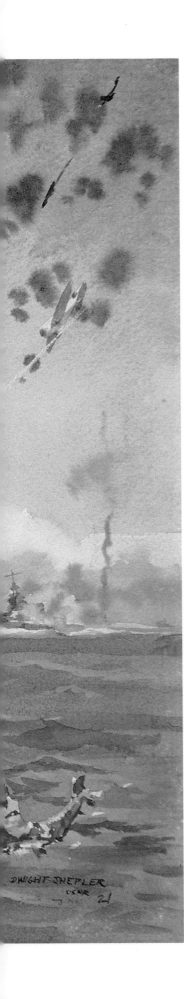

Battle of Santa Cruz— The First Air Attack

United States Navy

Dwight C. Shepler

MANY OF THE IMAGES IN THIS BOOK WERE CREATED LONG AFTER THE FACT, REQUIRING the artists to do considerable research. This wasn't the case with Dwight C. Shepler, an eyewitness to the battle of the Santa Cruz Islands on October 26, 1942. The battle was part of the overall campaign to maintain control of Guadalcanal, which U.S. Marines had invaded that August. Shepler was on board the light cruiser *San Juan*, which appears in the lower left corner of the painting. This painting depicts his vantage point during the battle.

The objective in the carrier-versus-carrier battles was to get one's own search planes off early, spot the enemy ships, then send a strike force to attack them before being attacked in turn. Before World War II, it was generally believed that aircraft carriers would act as support ships for the main combatants, which would be the battleships. By the summer and fall of 1942, the tables had been turned. The carriers unleashed the striking force, and it was up to the battleships, cruisers, and destroyers to maneuver in tandem with them and send up thousands of antiaircraft bullets at the attacking planes.

Vice Admiral Robert Ghormley, who was commander of the South Pacific Force, was a cautious man. He did not risk the battleship *Washington* to come to the aid of the *Hornet*'s task force, and that carrier was sunk during the Battle of the Santa Cruz Islands. However, the *Enterprise*, in the center of this painting, did survive thanks to all the gun power around her. A plane crashed onto the forecastle of the destroyer *Smith*, seen here to starboard of the *Enterprise*, and killed fifty-eight crewmen. The fire on her burning bow was extinguished when her skipper steamed into the high-frothing wake of the *South Dakota*, which shot down many planes that day to protect the carrier. The battleship was herself hit by a bomb that exploded atop a turret and sent shrapnel flying to the bridge, where it severely wounded Captain Thomas Gatch. Asked why he hadn't ducked, Gatch later explained, "The captain of a United States battleship considered it beneath his dignity to flop for a damned Japanese bomb."

The Fighting Hornet
United States Navy

Tom Lea

DURING HIS SIXTY-SIX DAYS ONBOARD THE *HORNET*, FROM AUGUST TO OCTOBER OF 1942, Tom Lea was able to roam the ship freely, make sketches, and get acquainted with members of the crew and the air group. Lea's portraits of the carrier's senior officers (opposite page) appeared in a feature published in the March 22, 1943, issue of *Life*.

In late October 1942, the skipper, Captain Charles Mason, said to Lea, "We don't think there's going to be any action here very soon—you better get back to Pearl with these drawings." He returned with sketches he had made as he witnessed the sinking of the carrier *Wasp* in mid-September. Because the loss of that ship was still classified, he refused to let customs officials see his drawings when he arrived in Hawaii. He was soon hauled in to see the Pacific Fleet public relations officer and, finally, the commander in chief himself, Chester Nimitz. As the admiral looked through the artist's drawings, he paused at a picture of the *Hornet* and said, "I hate to tell you this, but you lost your ship last night." Lea had not heard about the Santa Cruz battle, which occurred during his trip to Hawaii. Years later, he confessed, "Learning that the *Hornet* was gone was one of the most emotional things that happened to me in the war."

The *Hornet*, which had been commissioned on October 21, 1941, was a near sister of the *Yorktown* and the *Enterprise*. She differed slightly in having a more rounded shape to her bridge structure. In *The Fighting Hornet*, which appeared in *Life* in 1943, Lea reconstructed a scene of the carrier under attack. A 5-inch (13cm) antiaircraft gun blazes away in the foreground, while a Japanese aircraft plummets to the sea at the upper left and another crashes into the *Hornet*'s superstructure. The ship was fatally damaged by Japanese bombs on October 26, 1942, in the Battle of the Santa Cruz Islands, and she sank the following morning—just a little more than a year after her commissioning. George Murray, who skippered the *Enterprise* when she was with the *Hornet* on the Doolittle raid and at Midway, soon afterward became a rear admiral and commander of the *Hornet*'s task force.

In his time onboard, during the struggle for Guadalcanal, Lea essentially became one of the boys. He even flew as a rear-seat man with Lieutenant Commander Gus Widhelm, skipper of Scouting Eight, a Dauntless Squadron that was part of Commander Walt Rodee's Air Group Eight. (For a time, air groups matched the ship's hull number, in this case CV-8.)

The carrier's executive officer was Commander Apollo Soucek. On the *Hornet*'s final day, after she had been hit at Santa Cruz, Soucek toured the decks in company with Lieutenant Commander Francis Drake Foley, the ship's air operations officer. On the forecastle they saw a large Japanese bomb that was fuzed but had not exploded. They managed to roll it gingerly over the side and then jumped back. It hit the water without going off. Later they made their way to the bridge to tell Captain Charles Mason what they had seen. Among the scenes that Soucek and Foley had observed in their tour was that of two chaplains saying prayers and anointing the dead before their burial at sea. Then, after the dead had been so honored, Mason gave the order for the living to jump into the sea so they could be rescued and get on with the war.

COMMANDER TASK FORCE
Rear Admiral George D. Murray

USS HORNET, COMMANDING
Captain Charles P. Mason

AIR OFFICER
Commander M.E.A. Gouin

COMMANDER AIR GROUP
Commander Walter F. Rodee

SQUADRON COMMANDER
Lieut. Commander W.J. Widhelm

EXECUTIVE OFFICER
Commander Apollo Soucek
LEFT: The Exec goes to his battle station, carrying his life jacket, steel helmet, gas mask, and brief case.

Attack on the Hiei

United States Navy and Marine Corps

Robert Taylor

AFTER THE GREAT CARRIER BATTLES OF SEPTEMBER AND OCTOBER 1942, THE JAPANESE remained determined to recapture Guadalcanal and its vital airstrip, Henderson Field, named for Marine Major Lofton Henderson, who had been lost at Midway. On November 12, the Japanese sent a force of two battleships, one cruiser, fourteen destroyers, and eleven transports in an effort to bombard the island then deposit a force of soldiers ashore to recapture it from the U.S. Marines.

The "Tokyo Express," as the nocturnal efforts to retake Guadalcanal were known, was not able to carry out the operation as planned. Rear Admiral Richmond Kelly Turner, commander of the amphibious task force at Guadalcanal, dispatched a force of cruisers and destroyers to intercept the heavy surface ships. The result was a close-range slugfest that brought heavy damage to both sides. The Japanese battleship *Hiei* sustained more than eighty projectile hits and suffered a damaged steering gear. When Marine Captain Joe Foss flew a dawn patrol in his F4F the morning of November 13, he witnessed the injured ships of friend and foe.

As that Friday the 13th unfolded, the crippled *Hiei* served as a magnet for air operations by both sides. Historian John Lundstrom does a good job of describing the bustle of activity that day in his book *The First Team and the Guadalcanal Campaign*. Marine fliers came in from Henderson Field. The *Enterprise*, nearly 300 miles (483km) to the south, had a damaged elevator. She sent in a strike of F4Fs, SBDs, and TBFs, destined to attack the *Hiei* and then land on Guadalcanal. More than 200 miles (322km) north of Guadalcanal was the light carrier *Junyo*, which sent off her own strike. Still more planes came from the Japanese base at Rabaul on New Britain. The *Hiei*, a day after she was pounded by surface gunfire, received seven attack waves from the American fliers, including B-17s and P-39s of the Army Air Forces. Captain Foss participated in the fatal seventh wave, which delivered successful bomb and torpedo hits. That night the crew abandoned the *Hiei* and scuttled the ship. She was the first Japanese battleship sunk during the war.

The Kill

United States Navy

Robert Benny

IN THE EARLY MONTHS OF WORLD WAR II, GERMAN U-BOATS WERE DEVASTATING THE Atlantic shipping lanes. Even before the United States became an active combatant, the U.S. government was sending weapons, equipment, and supplies to Europe in order to prop up its ally, Britain, which by early 1941 was fighting Germany almost singlehandedly. Once the United States entered the war, U-boats began sinking its oil tankers and cargo ships in the seas off the East Coast. The two-ocean war had become a reality, and it took a while for the U.S. Navy to master antisubmarine warfare. One of the main tactics was the use of convoys, in which the cargo ships traveled together in formation and escort ships, such as destroyers, roved on the flanks like sheepdogs to protect against the German wolves. As an island nation, Britain depended greatly on its Atlantic lifeline, and it was stretched exceedingly thin by the depredations of the German submarines.

In the spring of 1943, the tide began to turn in the Allies' favor, particularly with the use of escort carriers, CVEs, that operated small air groups made up of Wildcat fighters and Avenger torpedo bombers. At first the CVEs joined with the destroyers in escorting convoys, and they were able to prey on the U-boats' vulnerabilities. In those days before nuclear power, submarines had to surface often to run their diesels and recharge storage batteries, as well as to resupply the crew with oxygen. In addition, German Admiral Karl Doenitz often used radio messages to direct the submarines' operations. The Allies were able both to decode the communications and to employ radio direction-finding to locate the submarines. Avengers, such as the one depicted in *The Kill*, attacked U-boats with depth bombs and homing torpedoes, which searched for submarines under the water. The planes could also strafe U-boats with machine guns, and the submarine crews often fought back, as the painting demonstrates.

After a time, the role of escort carriers and the destroyers they accompanied moved beyond the defensive mode of waiting for U-boats to approach convoys. CVEs such as the *Bogue* and the *Card* became the centerpieces of offensive hunter-killer groups that traveled to the known locations of German submarines.

An elevator lifts an Avenger up on deck, where plane handlers will spread and lock its folded wings before it is launched.

In his book *Hunter-Killer*, author William Y'Blood provides a vivid description of an attack: "Airborne radar, coupled with a powerful searchlight, was used with devastating effectiveness. One of the last sights some submariners saw was a brilliant light swooping down on them out of the night sky."

Practice Makes Perfect

United States Navy

Stan Stokes

T<small>HE SKYLINE OF</small> C<small>HICAGO PROVIDES AN UNLIKELY</small> backdrop as an SNJ trainer approaches an aircraft carrier. On the port side, a landing signal officer helps a novice pilot line up for an arrested landing as part of the training process that will qualify the pilot to join a fleet squadron. The ship is the training vessel *Wolverine*, built in 1913 as a coal-burning, paddle-wheel passenger ship.

As naval aviation expanded dramatically during the war, so did the need for pilots and training facilities. Captain Richard Whitehead came up with the idea of providing carrier qualifications onboard a ship in Lake Michigan, safely out of reach of attacking submarines. So in 1942 the old passenger cabins were stripped off the old ship, and a 500-foot (152m) flight deck was built atop her hull. An island structure was created on the starboard side to resemble the ones pilots would see on real carriers. The project was a success, so a year later a second ship was converted to a training carrier and became the USS *Sable*. The ships had neither catapults nor hangar decks.

Fledgling pilots practiced on runways ashore, which were marked to simulate carrier decks, before progressing to the paddle-wheel ships. The landing procedure was ingrained until the pilot was conditioned to carry it out. To Ensign Kent Lee, the first few times he landed on board the *Sable* were a blur of motion: he was so focused on what he had to do that he was unable to watch his surroundings. Only later, when the landing sequence became second nature, could he observe what was happening around him. All told, the two ships recorded more than 100,000 landings as they gave pilots the experience necessary to move on to the next step.

After planes landed and unhooked from the arresting wires, deck crews—like those shown here—prepared them to speed forward and take off. The pilots went through the drill again and again until each had made the required eight landings.

Ammunition Comes Aboard

United States Navy

William F. Draper

IN ONE SENSE, AN AIRCRAFT CARRIER IS A MOBILE, DENSELY POPULATED, FLOATING warehouse that runs an airport on the roof. The hundreds of occupants on a carrier run through a lot of consumables in the course of fighting a war. Frequently eliciting groans onboard a carrier in wartime were calls over the loudspeaker ordering a working party to move incoming cargo. The only variables in the announcement were the number of hands in the working party, the muster location, and the commodity to be carried.

Ammunition Comes Aboard depicts a ship that has just taken aboard a supply of green-and-yellow 5-inch (13cm) projectiles for its antiaircraft guns. They are lined up in rows on the hangar deck; a shirtless gunner's mate in dungarees directs some of his shipmates as they load the projectiles onto a pallet to be transported to the appropriate magazine for storage. When enemy planes approach, gun crews will move the projectiles from the magazine to an ammunition handling room and up a hoist to the gun. A cylindrical powder charge will load in behind the projectile, then the gun crew will fire it. Sometime later, another ammunition ship will come alongside and the crew will repeat the whole thing.

As part of its role as a storage facility, the hangar deck carries a spare SBD dive-bomber suspended from the overhead, as the Navy calls a ceiling. On the outer bulkhead are spare fuel tanks for F6F Hellcats, which would be suspended from the fuselage to provide extra range during a mission. The pilot could jettison the drop tank once it was empty, or even sooner if a burst of speed and maneuverability were needed.

On the right side of the painting, a maintenance man works on a Grumman TBF Avenger torpedo bomber, a real workhorse that fulfilled a variety of functions from 1942 onward. Capable of delivering glide-bombing attacks on ships or shore targets, performing photoreconnaissance missions, and attacking enemy submarines, it was a much more capable torpedo plane than the vulnerable TBD Devastator. One wag commented on the ruggedness of the Avenger: "Grumman built a mockup for it out of concrete and then made the real plane even heavier."

On Station

United States Navy

Tom Freeman

AFTER THE U.S. NAVY LOST THE *LEXINGTON*, THE *YORKTOWN*, THE *WASP*, AND THE *Hornet* in 1942, it needed time to build up its stable of fast carriers for the Central Pacific campaign that began in late 1943. The Navy would find new strength in the form of the large Essex-class ships, which spearheaded the amphibious island-hopping campaign toward the Japanese home islands in the latter half of the war. Construction of the *Essex* began at Newport News Shipbuilding in April 1941, and she was commissioned on the final day of 1942.

As the fast carriers demonstrated their ever increasing value during the war, the construction program was accelerated. Sixteen more ships of the same class joined the fleet during the conflict; one was the new *Yorktown*, shown here. The Navy originally planned to name the carrier *Bon Homme Richard* after John Paul Jones's Revolutionary War ship. But when the earlier *Yorktown* was lost at Midway, her name was given to the new carrier. Commissioned April 15, 1943, she was the second of the Essex class to join the fleet. She was commanded by the aggressive Captain Joseph J. "Jocko" Clark, who took her into her first combat action when her fighters and bombers struck Japanese installations on Marcus Island on August 31, 1943.

Though not identified by name at the time, the *Yorktown*'s operations became familiar to moviegoers in 1944 with the release of a film titled *The Fighting Lady*. It was directed by Louis de Rochemont, who employed the newly created color film stock to great effect, conveying both shipboard action and scenes filmed from the planes of her air group. At the following year's Academy Awards presentation, the movie won the Oscar for best documentary feature. Many years later, during the twilight of her active service, the *Yorktown* portrayed a Japanese carrier in the 1970 movie *Tora! Tora! Tora!* She was decommissioned that same year. On October 13, 1975, the 200th anniversary of the establishment of the Navy, she was dedicated as the centerpiece of a naval museum at Patriot's Point, near Charleston, South Carolina. It is an ideal resting place for a ship whose name evokes the founding of the nation.

Halsey's Surprise

United States Navy

Craig Kodera

Joe Clifton, skipper of Fighter Squadron 12, indulges in ice cream (a lifelong passion of his) after returning from the raid on Rabaul. This photo appears in *USS Saratoga, CV-3*, author John Fry's beautifully illustrated history of the ship's long career.

CAPTAIN WILLIAM F. HALSEY, JR., EARNED HIS WINGS AS A NAVAL AVIATOR AT THE AGE of fifty-two. A 1925 law mandated that aviation officers command aircraft carriers, so his training qualified him to take command of the *Saratoga* in 1934. By the time war began in 1941, he had moved up to become the senior naval aviation admiral. He commanded the task force for the April 1942 raid on Tokyo, but a skin ailment would keep him out of the Midway action.

Halsey's October 1942 arrival in the South Pacific had energized the desperate U.S. forces in their struggle to maintain control of Guadalcanal. During the ensuing slow march north up the Solomons chain, the Allies' principal weapons were amphibious forces, cruisers, and destroyers. On November 1, 1943, Halsey sent Task Force 38, built around the old *Saratoga* and the new light carrier *Princeton*, to support the invasion of Bougainville in the northern Solomons. Then came a report that the Japanese had moved eight cruisers, four destroyers, and dozens of aircraft into Rabaul, whence they could pose a major threat to the amphibious shipping at Bougainville. Reluctantly, Halsey dispatched Task Force 38 to conduct a raid against Rabaul on November 5. Sending the attackers in to face land-based Japanese aircraft was a grave risk. As he wrote in his postwar memoir, "This was the most desperate emergency that confronted me in my entire term [in the South Pacific] . . . I sincerely expected both air groups to be cut to pieces and both carriers to be stricken if not lost."

Halsey's Surprise depicts the launch from the *Saratoga* in progress, with two SBDs already overhead. Despite Halsey's doubts, the American strike succeeded brilliantly. Commander "Jumping Joe" Clifton's Hellcats from the *Saratoga* stuck to the attacking dive-bombers and torpedo planes like glue to protect them from the Japanese fighters. The Japanese ships, caught without warning, maneuvered frantically in the harbor at Rabaul to try to escape the U.S. bombs and torpedoes. Japanese antiaircraft fire was intense, but only a handful of aircraft from the ninety-seven–plane strike group failed to return. They inflicted damage on six Japanese cruisers, while the American ships escaped unharmed. The risk had paid off, and Bougainville was safe.

Refueling Destroyers

United States Navy

Mitchell Jamieson

The USS *Lexington* refuels from a tanker near the Marshall Islands in November 1943.

BEANS, BULLETS AND BLACK OIL, WRITTEN BY COMMODORE Worrall R. Carter and published in 1953, described the U.S. Navy's activities in the Pacific in World War II. In a few words, his title summed up the major logistical needs of a fleet operating over vast stretches of ocean. Indeed, Japan's recognition that it needed supplies of oil and other raw materials had been one of the driving forces behind its militant expansionist policy of the 1930s. Unlike today's Navy ships, which run on either nuclear fuel or light petroleum distillates, the steam-powered warships of World War II burned a much heavier black substance known as Navy special fuel oil.

Those who attempted early carrier actions in World War II recognized that the requirement for fuel dictated just what operations were feasible. Fortunately for the U.S. effort, the cautious Japanese Vice Admiral Chuichi Nagumo had elected on December 7, 1941, not to make a third, late-morning strike that could have wiped out the fuel tank farm at Pearl Harbor. Had he done so, the American comeback would have been even more difficult than it was. Even so, fleet oilers were in short supply. For the most part, these were civilian oil tankers converted for Navy use by the installation of rigs, allowing for hoses to be passed to ships that steamed in alongside for underway refueling. Oilers provided the carriers with both the heavy black fuel for the ship's boilers and the high-octane aviation gasoline for the carrier's aircraft.

Operations in 1942 were hampered by the sinking of the oilers *Pecos, Neches,* and *Neosho* by the Japanese, so in the war's early months, the warships often came back to Pearl in between operations to be resupplied. As the war progressed, though, American industrial productivity built up the number of oilers and other supply ships. The U.S. Pacific Fleet became a truly mobile striking force, able to stay at sea for weeks at a time by being resupplied with the consumables of war. And those warships were thirsty as they went about their high-speed operations. Rather than thinking in terms of miles per gallon, as auto drivers do, the shipboard engineers thought in terms of dozens of gallons of fuel for each mile steamed. Those needing to take a drink most often were the destroyers, such as the one shown here alongside an escort carrier, a CVE. Because their fuel tanks were much smaller than those of the carriers, the destroyers had to refuel every few days, sometimes directly from oilers, but more often from large combatants such as carriers, cruisers, and battleships. Four escort carriers—the *Santee,* the *Sangamon,* the *Chenango,* and the *Suwanee*—had been built originally as tankers before having flight decks slapped on top. As a result, they carried a huge supply of fuel, both for themselves and for ships that needed refueling.

Hangar Deck of Carrier
United States Navy

William F. Draper

DURING OPERATIONS AT SEA, THE HANGAR DECK WAS A BUSY PLACE THAT SERVED MANY functions, foremost of which was the storage and maintenance of aircraft between flight operations. Though it could be closed off with metal curtains that rolled up and down, it was often an open, airy place. In fact, in the early ships of the Essex class, designers even built in a provision to launch planes from hangar-deck catapults that ran perpendicular to the main axis of the carrier. Another emergency provision was the ability to launch planes off the stern when the carrier was backing down, in case the bow was damaged. Though the second *Yorktown* (CV-10) tested these experimental features, neither was widely used.

The hangar deck was one of the two main social centers for crew members onboard a World War II carrier; the other was the mess deck, where they ate. Sailors gathered in the hangar deck to watch movies, play basketball, and just shoot the breeze with shipmates. Onboard the first *Yorktown* (CV-5), as Robert Cressman relates in his excellent book *That Gallant Ship*, the hangar deck was the site of an unusual auction. After prolonged operations in early 1942, the ship was down to one last T-bone steak onboard. The rare treat was carried around the ship by a Marine guard, accompanied by the ship's band. Crew members bid on portions of the steak and the winners were the envy of their shipmates as they claimed their prize. One of the elevators served as a platform, slightly raised above the level of the hangar deck itself, much in the manner of a boxing ring in an arena. On April 10, 1942, the three winners sat at a table on the elevator and claimed their prize. Fourteen-year-old John Underwood, an enlisted member of Fighter Squadron 42, donned woman's clothing and served as "waitress." Surrounding the raised platform in the hangar deck were the shipmates who vicariously tasted each bite as it went down.

Three lucky crew members dine on the *Yorktown*'s last T-bone steak at a meal served in the ship's hangar deck in April 1942.

Crash Landing

United States Navy

William F. Draper

LANDING AN AIRPLANE ON THE DECK OF A CARRIER at sea is a dangerous procedure that requires considerable skill. The pilot must bring his plane in at a speed just above that at which the engine will stall. During World War II, the landing signal officer on the port side at the carrier's stern used paddles to signal a pilot on the quality of his approach. If he was coming in too high, too low, or too fast, the LSO gave him a waveoff and sent him back up into the landing circle to come around and try again. A tailhook hangs down from the back end of each carrier plane, and, as the plane touches down, the pilot tries to snag one of the cross-deck arresting wires that will bring him to an abrupt stop.

Lieutenant Walter Chewning, Jr., climbs up the fuselage of a burning F6F Hellcat to rescue pilot Ensign Byron Johnson from the cockpit after his plane crash-landed on the flight deck of the *Enterprise* in 1945.

But not all the landings were successful, as these images vividly demonstrate. In *Crash Landing*, a broken plane has smashed into the aft end of the island on the starboard side of the new *Yorktown* during strikes against the Palau Islands on March 12, 1944. Sometimes the incoming planes missed the arresting wires and went crashing into the barrier that had been stretched across the deck to prevent further damage to the planes parked forward on the flight deck.

The first carrier *Yorktown* also suffered mishaps before being sunk in the Battle of Midway. As the ship was preparing to sortie for that encounter, Lieutenant Commander John Thach, commanding officer of Fighting Squadron Three, quickly accepted the offer of his friend, Lieutenant Commander Don Lovelace, to serve as his executive officer. But, as author Robert Cressman recounts in *That Gallant Ship*, a history of the *Yorktown,* tragedy ensued. On Memorial Day 1942, the squadron flew aboard ship in its F4F Wildcats to set out for Midway. Lovelace, flying in squadron plane number 13, caught a wire upon landing, disengaged, and then taxied forward. The next pilot, Ensign R.C. Evans, came in behind, missed the wires, and flew over the barrier. The propeller of his Wildcat chewed into the cockpit of Lovelace's plane and killed the executive officer before he had a chance to fight in the battle for which he had been preparing his entire professional life.

Up to the Flight Deck

United States Navy

William F. Draper

SPACE WAS AT A PREMIUM ONBOARD THE WORLD WAR II CARRIERS, EVEN THE LARGE ones of the Essex class. As a result, most of the carrier planes were designed with folding wings so they could be parked closer together, thus taking up less space on the flight deck or hangar deck. Before a launch, the wings would be spread and locked into place. In *Up to the Flight Deck*, a group of dungaree-clad sailors maneuver an Avenger, with wings folded over the fuselage, onto the elevator for a trip to the flight deck. At that time, as it still is today, the job of a plane handler was a difficult one, involving both considerable physical effort and danger.

In World War II, carrier elevators were located on a ship's centerline, significantly complicating flight operations. The elevators had to be up to their deck-level position for landings and takeoffs. It wasn't until the 1950s that carrier innovations brought about an improvement in the situation. Deck-edge elevators permitted the raising and lowering of planes without interfering with landing and takeoff operations. In addition, angled flight decks enabled aircraft to land at the stern without posing a hazard to planes that were parked forward on the flight deck.

Moored atop the wood-covered flight deck, wings folded back, F6F Hellcats and TBF Avengers await action. Beyond them, on the ship's stern, the planes are parked farther apart because their wings are still extended.

100 USS Harder Rescues Ensign John Galvin

USS Harder Rescues Ensign John Galvin

United States Navy

Tom Freeman

Not only the most successful American submarine skipper during the war, in terms of Japanese ships sunk, Commander Richard O'Kane, commanding officer of the *Tang*, was also an expert at rescuing downed pilots. Kane is shown here at center surrounded by aviators his boat pulled from the water.

WHEN THE CENTRAL PACIFIC CAMPAIGN BEGAN IN LATE 1943, THE COMMANDER OF the fast carrier task force was Rear Admiral Charles Pownall. Because Pownall was concerned about his pilots' welfare, he made an arrangement with the submarine force to provide lifeguard services in the vicinity of carrier strikes. A prime beneficiary of this setup was Ensign John R. Galvin, pilot of an F6F Hellcat in Fighter Squadron Eight, flying from the carrier *Bunker Hill*. On April Fool's Day 1944, he was part of a strike group that attacked the Japanese-held island of Woleai so that the aircraft there could not hamper upcoming U.S. amphibious operations on New Guinea. In his colorfully named memoir, *Salvation for a Doomed Zoomie,* Galvin described the courageous operation by which the men of the submarine USS *Harder*, under Commander Sam Dealey, rescued him and saved his life.

Galvin explained that he was shot down because he strayed from his flight of Hellcats to strafe a Betty bomber on a runway. He managed to parachute from his plane, land in the water offshore, and swim to a coral reef. His squadron mates flew overhead to protect him and also sent a radio message that brought the *Harder* to his vicinity. Dealey essentially had to run the submarine bow aground on the coral reef to get close enough to attempt a rescue. Strong swimmers from the submarine retrieved the injured, exhausted pilot. After hoisting him into a raft, the men of the *Harder* tried to pull him in. Unfortunately, a cruiser floatplane also trying to help Galvin inadvertently cut the towline, necessitating still more heroism on the part of submarine crew members. They finally brought the aviator aboard. Such rescues gave carrier pilots a boost in morale because they had confidence they would be saved whenever possible.

Scramble for the Marianas

United States Navy

Nicolas Trudgian

ON JUNE 15, 1944, U.S. MARINES SLAMMED ASHORE on the invasion beaches of the island of Saipan in the Marianas, bringing the American presence ever closer to Japan. At the direction of Admiral Raymond Spruance, commander of the Fifth Fleet, the American carrier force and its escorts were, in effect, tethered in the vicinity of Saipan and the neighboring island of Guam. The Japanese carrier force, which had seen only limited action since the Guadalcanal campaign of late 1942, no longer had the cream-of-the-crop pilots of two years earlier. Nonetheless, their carriers came in force to contest the landings in the Marianas. The Japanese carriers benefited from the ability to stay out of range: their planes could land on Guam and refuel rather than having to make a round trip on a load of gas.

The Americans, however, had advantages of their own. One was superior radar equipment to detect the incoming planes. They also had a talented group of lieutenants who acted as fighter director officers. These men managed the complex business of assessing threats and following up with radio instructions to the fighters, sending them out to intercept the enemy. In this painting, Lieutenant (j.g.) Alex Vraciu of Fighter Squadron 16 takes off from the carrier *Lexington* on June 19. As the tiny flags near his cockpit indicate, he has already shot down twelve enemy planes. Vraciu's gunnery that day was superb. When he completed the mission and landed back aboard the Task Force 58 flagship, he smiled in triumph as he held up six fingers to indicate the number of planes he had shot down in an eight-minute span. Many of his fellow Hellcat pilots also added to their bag that day—more than 300 Japanese planes fell.

Lieutenant Commander Paul Buie (center), commanding officer of the *Lexington*'s Fighter Squadron 16, coaches his pilots before a mission. After the June 19 battle, he heard one of them compare the aerial slaughter to an old-fashioned "turkey shoot." Since then that battle has been known as the "Great Marianas Turkey Shoot."

Mission Beyond Darkness

United States Navy

Robert Taylor

ON THE NIGHT OF JUNE 18, 1944, AS THE JAPANESE fleet approached from the west to contest the American invasion of Saipan, Vice Admiral Marc Mitscher was in command of Task Force 58. His chief of staff was an aggressive destroyer officer, Captain Arleigh Burke. At Burke's urging, Mitscher asked Vice Admiral Willis A. Lee, commander of the fleet's battleships, if he wanted a surface gun battle at night. Lee declined because his ships didn't have sufficient experience maneuvering together, and Admiral Raymond Spruance endorsed Lee's decision. He was concerned that the Japanese fleet might make an end around and attack the invasion forces on the beachhead at Saipan.

At midafternoon on June 20, the day after the "turkey shoot," search planes from Task Force 58 finally found the Japanese fleet 300 miles (483km) to the west. Not wanting to let the Japanese escape, Mitscher ordered more than 200 fighters, dive-bombers, and torpedo planes to strike the enemy. He knew the risks; the distance involved was considerable and pilots lacked night landing experience. The U.S. planes sank the carrier *Hiyo* and damaged four others. They also sank two oilers and damaged the battleship *Haruna*, a nemesis since early in the war. Mitscher then took another risk by ordering his ships to turn on their searchlights and point them skyward as beacons to guide the carrier planes on their long flight home. Even so, the result was a mad scramble as some planes landed on their own ships, some landed aboard others, and still others had to ditch into the Philippine Sea as their fuel tanks ran dry. *Mission Beyond Darkness* depicts the scene as pilot Lieutenant Ralph Yaussi and his rear gunner, James Curry, kill time on their SB2C dive-bomber as they wait to be picked up by the destroyer *Anthony* nearby. In the background, her searchlight beam reaching up, is Mitscher's flagship, the carrier *Lexington*.

Vice Admiral Marc Mitscher, commander of Task Force 58, in a portrait by combat artist Albert K. Murray.

Ready Room

United States Navy

William F. Draper

ONBOARD A CARRIER IN WARTIME WAS A hierarchy of ranks and rates. At the top of the pyramid, though not necessarily the highest in rank, were the aviators. Because they were the elite, pilots had access to special compartments known as ready rooms, in which they spent a great deal of their time between flights. Each squadron had its own, and the term "ready room" came from the fact that preflight briefings were held in these rooms to prepare the aviators for their missions. But, as William F. Draper demonstrates in *Ready Room,* these compartments were also places of relaxation and camaraderie. There the pilots could read magazines, write letters, play cards, and engage in chitchat.

Ensign Don Engen, the smiling young flier in the lower left corner, awaits a briefing in the ready room of Bombing Squadron 19 (VB-19) onboard the carrier *Lexington* in 1944. Note the parachute packs hanging on the bulkhead. Engen's memoir provides an excellent description of life onboard a carrier. Referring to the cramped bunkroom, he wrote, "Boys' town was for sleeping, not living, and we spent most of our time in our respective ready rooms, which were blessedly air conditioned." The rest of the ship was not.

Dressed in the standard uniform of wash khakis with long-sleeved shirts, the pilots were ready to go to general-quarters stations at a moment's notice and could simply pull on their flight suits when it was time for a mission. Aviators wore soft-cloth helmets and goggles, a far cry from the hard plastic helmets of today.

When an operation was imminent, the squadron members received briefings based on teletype reports that came in from the ship's air operations office. As pilot Don Engen wrote in his memoir, *Wings and Warriors,* "The teletype machine, with its 3-by-3-foot [0.9-by-0.9km], illuminated, yellow, translucent cloth screen, was our link to the world through air ops; it seemingly controlled our lives." The pilots listened to the preflight reports while sitting in padded, lean-back seats. Under each seat was a navigation plotting board, for the ability to find one's way over open ocean to a target—and then back to the carrier—was a vital skill for sea-based aviators. The last thing pilots learned before heading to the flight deck to man their planes was the position and intended movements of the carrier so they would know where to meet her later.

After a mission concluded and the aircraft were safely back onboard, the pilots again trooped into the ready room, this time for a debriefing with an air combat intelligence officer, who recorded recollections while they were still fresh and pieced together the various pilot reports. Aviators also filled out yellow aircraft maintenance sheets so that deficiencies could be fixed before it was time to fly again. And then it was time to unwind, perhaps with a nip of alcohol (either official or contraband), which was so helpful after times of stress.

© 89 T E D   W I L B U R

108 HIGH SIDE ATTACK OVER LEYTE GULF

High Side Attack Over Leyte Gulf

United States Navy

Ted Wilbur

The Japanese rising sun flag insignias emblazoning the fuselage of Commander David McCampbell's aircraft (nicknamed "Minsi III" after a girlfriend) vividly testify to the combat success of this renowned American flying ace.

AMONG THE MOST CELEBRATED U.S. NAVAL AVIATORS OF WORLD WAR II WAS Commander David McCampbell. He racked up a remarkable score—thirty-four aerial victories against Japanese planes—and the honor of being the U.S. Navy's top fighter ace of the war.

On October 24, 1944, during the Battle of Leyte Gulf, the *Essex* launched a fighter sweep. McCampbell did not go because he was slated to command the air group, not act as a fighter pilot. But then the ship got word of an incoming raid of land-based Japanese planes from the island of Luzon. This time the ship needed fighters in the air for defense, and McCampbell was called on to go, even though his Hellcat was only partially fueled. He climbed to altitude with his wingman, Lieutenant (j.g.) Roy Rushing, a naval reservist. They headed off slightly north of west, seeking to intercept enemy planes only a bit more than twenty miles (32km) away. As they and other Hellcats from the *Essex* approached, the Japanese fighters went into a Lufbery Circle, each following the tail of the plane ahead for mutual protection.

McCampbell and Rushing waited patiently, and the skipper even lit up a cigarette to pass the time. When the Japanese finally broke the circle and tried to hightail it for Luzon, the Americans pounced, swooping down from their altitude advantage. Rushing, a fine wingman, stayed very close to McCampbell; the two Hellcat pilots communicated with hand signals to cut down on radio traffic. They made run after run with their .50-caliber machine guns, and McCampbell made pencil marks on his dashboard to indicate the number of Japanese shot down. At mission's end, he had flamed nine planes with his gunnery and had two more probables; Rushing had shot down six for a total of fifteen. Commander McCampbell was awarded the Medal of Honor for the day's mission.

Carrier Down

United States Navy

R.G. Smith

AFTER 1942 THE U.S. NAVY LOST ONLY ONE FAST CARRIER DURING THE REMAINDER OF the war. That was the CVL *Princeton*, which was originally intended to be the light cruiser *Tallahassee*. Instead, she acquired a flight deck and an air group and became part of Task Group 38.3 while supporting the invasion of Leyte. On the morning of October 24, 1944, a Japanese Judy glide bomber emerged through a hole in the overhanging clouds and dropped a 550-pound (250kg) bomb on the *Princeton*'s flight deck. It penetrated down three decks and exploded, sparking raging fires in the hangar deck. Torpedoes on the TBM Avengers exploded, sending both of the ship's flight deck elevators flying skyward.

The destroyer *Irwin* came alongside to render help and rescue crew members, and later the light cruiser *Birmingham* provided firefighting assistance. The cruiser had to leave for a while because of concern about a possible submarine threat. Soon after she returned, the after end of the *Princeton* erupted as her torpedo storage area blew up. The force of the explosion blew across the deck of the *Birmingham* and caused horrendous personnel casualties. With the carrier still blazing and no other ship able to take her in tow, the task group commander, Rear Admiral Ted Sherman, reluctantly ordered her destroyed. The *Irwin*'s torpedoes ran erratically, so it was left to the cruiser *Reno* to deliver the coup de grâce late that afternoon. Her two torpedoes struck home and exploded, sending debris more than a thousand feet (305m) in the air. The *Princeton* sank soon after.

The wounded included Captain John Hoskins, who lost his right foot when the *Princeton* was damaged. He had been due to take command of the carrier. After receiving an artificial foot, he became the first skipper of the new carrier *Princeton*, which was commissioned soon after the war ended. Among those killed on board the *Birmingham* was the cruiser's first lieutenant, who had married shortly before the war but had been able to spend little time with his bride. His widow, Betsy Shaw, has written a poignant memoir describing her feelings at being separated by war from her new husband, and then the sense of loss after his sudden death.

USS Langley at Leyte
United States Navy

Mark Churms

DURING THE EARLY PART OF THE WAR, WHEN IT BECAME APPARENT THAT AIRCRAFT carriers were going to play a substantial role in the war in the Pacific, President Franklin D. Roosevelt ordered a number of ships that were being built as light cruisers to be converted to aircraft carriers. One of these was the planned cruiser *Fargo*, under construction at the New York Shipbuilding Corporation in Camden, New Jersey. As was the case with eight sister ships, she received a flight deck in place of the planned superstructure, and was equipped with four smokestacks on the starboard side in place of the two amidships she would have received as a cruiser. As a carrier, she was renamed the *Langley* in honor of the first U.S. carrier, which had been sunk in 1942.

The nine converted ships—designated CVLs, or light carriers—had limited capabilities. Though the Independence-class ships had the speed to keep up

with the large Essex-class attack carriers, they had nowhere near the airplane capacity. The *Langley* and her sisters could accommodate a load of approximately thirty planes apiece, compared with three times that many for the large carriers. The CVLs also featured relatively short and narrow flight decks. Lieutenant Ray Hawkins, a pilot in the sister ship *Cabot*, eventually got used to the narrow landing area on the stern of his Independence-class carrier. When he had occasion to land on one of the larger, wider ships of the Essex class, he jokingly asked whether he should use the port or starboard runway.

Shown here, the light carrier *Langley* launches a Hellcat fighter, while her sister ship *Princeton* burns in the background on October 24, 1944, during the Sibuyan Sea portion of the Battle of Leyte Gulf. The *Princeton* was the only CVL lost during the war.

Battle of Leyte Gulf

United States Navy

James Dietz

ON OCTOBER 25, 1944, ADMIRAL WILLIAM HALSEY TOOK HIS THIRD FLEET NORTH to attack a group of Japanese carriers. He had no idea that the carriers were sacrificial decoys, deliberately designed to lure him away from San Bernardino Strait, thus enabling the Japanese center force under Vice Admiral Takeo Kurita to break through and attack the American transports at Leyte. What resulted was a David-versus-Goliath confrontation. On watch that morning on the bridge of the destroyer *Franks* was Quartermaster Mike Bak. As he looked out from his ship, he was astonished to see what looked like toothpicks poking above the horizon. He soon realized they were the masts of large Japanese warships, steaming ever closer to the defending force of small American vessels—destroyers and escort carriers. The *Franks* and other ships fishtailed back and forth trying to elude the heavy shells falling all around them.

Bravery was widespread that morning among the destroyer skippers, who boldly took their ships in close among the Japanese to fire their guns and torpedoes at vessels that were far more heavily armed. In the upper right corner of Dietz's *Battle of Leyte Gulf* is the battleship *Yamato*, armed with 18.1-inch (46cm) guns. The destroyers' biggest guns were 5 inches (13 cm). In the foreground is a destroyer with a gun crew manning 40-millimeters and a bank of torpedo tubes just beyond. In the center, another destroyer blasts away with her 5-inchers. Particularly noteworthy that day at Leyte were the *Heermann*, whose skipper was Commander Amos Hathaway; the *Johnston*, under Commander Ernest E. Evans; and the *Samuel B. Roberts*, skippered by Lieutenant Commander R.W. Copeland. Evans was lost with his ship and was awarded a posthumous Medal of Honor.

The Final Hour

United States Navy

Carl G. Evers

THE COURAGEOUS AMERICAN DESTROYER SKIPPERS DID WHAT THEY COULD TO DETER the heavily armed Japanese warships from devastating the force off the island of Samar. They and the escort carriers of Rear Admiral Tommy Sprague's Taffy Three task force were left to deal with the Japanese giants that should have been faced by Vice Admiral Willis Lee's fast battleships. But Lee's ships had gone north with Admiral Halsey, missing the battle entirely.

As soon as their predicament became clear on the morning of October 25, 1944, the escort carriers sent their air groups aloft to do whatever they could to deter the oncoming Japanese. Planes from the CVEs (including the USS *Gambier Bay*, shown here) got some help from shore-based aircraft, but many of those were handicapped because they did not have sufficient weaponry. The Avengers fired their entire supply of torpedoes and the Wildcats made strafing runs to try to take out personnel who were topside on Japanese ships. But even these heroic efforts were all for naught once the .50-caliber bullets ran out.

Some courageous pilots made dry runs on the advancing enemy ships in an attempt to force them to change course and to distract them, and thus compromise the accuracy of their guns. The combined measures of the destroyers and the jeep carriers were only partly successful, because they were so completely overwhelmed in terms of firepower.

Here the *Gambier Bay* is surrounded by the multicolored splashes of falling Japanese projectiles. (The heavy projectiles were loaded with dye, using different colors for each ship. The ships doing the firing could then ascertain from the colors where their own projectiles were falling.) The Japanese chased the plucky carrier with their shots for twenty-five minutes as her skipper, Captain W.V.R. Vieweg, ably steered her out of the way. But when the Japanese got within 10,000 yards (9,144m), they found the range and pummeled the carrier, eventually sinking her. One of the *Gambier Bay* aviators who survived was Lieutenant Commander Fred "Buzz" Borries, who had been a star athlete at the Naval Academy in the mid-1930s. He had opted to go into aviation because he believed the era of the big guns was over. Now, ironically, his carrier was sunk by big guns.

Admiral William Halsey onboard the battleship *New Jersey*, which was his flagship during the Battle of Leyte Gulf. His decision to chase decoy carriers to the north left the *Gambier Bay* and other small ships exposed to attack.

Too Close For Comfort

United States Navy

Tom Freeman

IN THE SPRING OF 1942, SEVENTEEN-YEAR-OLD DON ENGEN OF CALIFORNIA SOUGHT to enter the Naval Academy but failed the chemistry portion of the entrance exam and was not admitted. If he *had* gained admission, he would have spent the bulk of the war in Annapolis, Maryland—but fate had other plans. Instead, he enlisted in the Navy's aviation cadet program on the day in May when he turned eighteen. In June of 1943, twelve days after his nineteenth birthday, he was commissioned an ensign and awarded his wings as a naval aviator. Also in his graduating class was future President George Bush. En route to combat, in September, Engen married his girlfriend, Mary Baker—an opportunity that would have been denied to a Naval Academy midshipman.

By autumn 1944, Engen and his rear-seat gunner, Aviation Radioman Ted Stevenson, were flying in an SB2C-3 Helldiver from the carrier *Lexington*. After the Japanese carrier force was sighted northeast of the Philippines, the carrier air groups of Task Force 38 took part in what became known as the Battle of Cape Engano. Engen's plane was part of the strike group sent to attack on October 25. Once over the target, Engen put his plane into a near-vertical dive and planted a bomb on the deck of the *Zuikaku*, which sank that day. She had been the last surviving veteran of the six carriers whose planes struck Pearl Harbor in 1941. The antiaircraft fire was so intense that Engen took his plane as close to the water as he could to get below the hail of bullets. In his escape he flew the Helldiver right in front of the bow of the hybrid battleship-with-a-flight-deck *Hyuga*, close enough to see the rust streaks on her anchor. Stevenson sent a hail of machine gun bullets toward the Japanese officers who stood on deck in their formal uniforms. On a later flight that day, Engen attacked the *Hyuga* herself; the battleship was damaged but survived.

Following that combat experience as a junior officer, Engen went on to become a test pilot, skipper of the carrier *America*, a vice admiral, head of the Federal Aviation Administration, and, finally, director of the Smithsonian Institution's National Air and Space Museum.

Young Don Engen, helmet in hand and knife at his belt, poses in his flight gear.

Corsair

United States Navy

Ted Wilbur

THE F4U CORSAIR FIGHTER WAS A HOT PLANE, WITH A MAXIMUM SPEED OF MORE THAN 400 miles per hour (644kph); and it was a versatile one, eventually able to carry 1,000-pound (454kg) bombs, rockets, and, of course, the .50-caliber machine guns that made it an excellent plane for air-to-air combat and the strafing of ground targets. But it had its faults, too. The F4U had difficulties in early carrier suitability tests: its long nose created visibility problems for the pilots, and the stiffness of the landing gear led to bounces on hard-deck landings. Thus the first production-model Corsairs were sent to land-based Marine Corps fighter squadrons in 1943. In 1944, after further carrier suitability tests, F4Us reported to sea-based squadrons in both the Royal Navy and the U.S. Navy.

As was the case throughout the U.S. armed services in World War II, the prewar pilots served as mentors for the thousands of young men who were civilians until joining up for service after the attack on Pearl Harbor. It was up to the veteran instructor pilots in various training commands to turn the newcomers into capable aviators. Typical of these trainees was Bill Cantrell, who graduated from Drury College in Springfield, Missouri, in 1942, and entered the pipeline of training in which he flew ever more challenging aircraft. Then, as now, the Navy provided flight training for all three sea services: the Navy, the Marine Corps, and the Coast Guard.

When he had received the required number of up-checks and had qualified for his aviator wings, Cantrell opted to become a Marine second-lieutenant. He flew an F4U in VMF-114 during the later stages of the Pacific war. He and his squadron mates savored the fact that they were more accurate at hitting their bombing targets than their high-flying counterparts in the Army Air Forces. And Cantrell took particular satisfaction in using his machine guns and bombs to provide close air support for his fellow Marines when they battled an enemy on the ground in such places as Peleliu in the Palau Islands. Cantrell was wounded in action, recuperated, got married, and after the war returned to Springfield to pursue a career in the retail clothing business. Like many of his contemporaries, he helped win the war and then got on with his life.

Heading Home

United States Navy

Hugh Polder

THE REPLACEMENT FOR THE SBD DAUNTLESS WAS A NEWER, BIGGER BOMBER: THE Curtiss SB2C Helldiver, nicknamed the "beast" by its pilots because of its size and handling characteristics. It was often difficult to land and had a tendency to float over the arresting wires. Moreover, the first Helldivers used in trials had multiple mechanical problems, but progress could not be halted. The rugged SB2C gained fans of its own as time passed, particularly because it could carry a heavier bomb load than the SBD.

In *Heading Home*, two Helldivers return to their ship, the new *Yorktown*, after a successful mission against the Japanese. The *Yorktown* and the rest of Task Force 38 were extremely busy during the Philippine campaign of January 1945 and before the February strikes against the Japanese home islands and the invasion of Iwo Jima. In January the carrier's Air Group Three bolstered the invasion at Lingayen Gulf, on the island of Luzon in the Philippines, and supported the attacks on Formosa, the Chinese coast, Hong Kong, Hainan, Okinawa, and other locations.

In addition to the land attacks, Admiral Halsey took the Third Fleet into the South China Sea as he sought to destroy the Japanese diversionary force that had played him for a chump at Leyte. He was particularly eager to catch the half-battleships *Ise* and *Hyuga*, but they managed to elude him as they kept moving and finally returned to Japan in February. Even so, planes from the *Yorktown* and other ships of Task Force 38 inflicted considerable damage. On January 12, in the vicinity of what was then called Indochina—later Vietnam—American fliers sank forty-four Japanese ships, including fifteen warships.

Avenger
United States Navy

Ted Wilbur

Future President George Bush in a photo taken by Robert Stinnett, a *San Jacinto* shipmate who later wrote a book, *George Bush: His World War II Years,* describing Bush's wartime exploits. The young pilot, outfitted with a parachute harness, inflatable Mae West life jacket, and dye marker, is making notes on an intelligence bulletin.

FRESH OUT OF PREP SCHOOL, GEORGE BUSH ENLISTED IN THE NAVAL RESERVE ON JUNE 12, 1942, his eighteenth birthday. He soon entered the V-5 program to train as a naval aviation cadet. On June 9, 1943, after learning to fly in a Stearman N2S trainer and getting advanced instruction in an SNJ Texan, Bush received his ensign's commission and the gold wings of a naval aviator. Not yet nineteen, he was one of the U.S. Navy's youngest pilots ever.

Combat duty took Ensign Bush to Torpedo Squadron 51, which operated TBM Avengers from the light carrier *San Jacinto.* He got into action with bombing runs on the islands of Saipan and Guam during the Marianas invasion in June 1944. On June 19, the day of the great "turkey shoot," Bush was on deck in his plane "Barbara," named for his fiancée Barbara Pierce. Japanese Zeros attacked, so he had to launch to avoid being hit. A catapult launched his plane, but soon after takeoff the engine began to sputter. His oil pressure was low and he was forced to ditch the plane and its crew in the sea. The destroyer *Clarence K. Bronson* rescued the men, but the plane was lost.

Subsequently, Bush was involved in photo-intelligence operations with a new "Barbara"; the camera shot through a hole just below the number 2 painted on the side of the fuselage. On September 2, 1944, he and his radioman and turret gunner were due for a bombing mission on the island of Chichi Jima in the Bonins. Lieutenant (j.g.) Ted White, the squadron ordnance officer, asked to go along to familiarize himself with the plane's operations, and thus displaced a very disappointed gunner, Leo Nadeau. Bush dropped his four 500-pound (227kg) bombs over the target, but antiaircraft gunnery hit his Avenger and set it on fire. Bush and one other crewman bailed out. The young aviator banged against the plane, suffered a head wound, and ripped his parachute, but managed to land safely in the water. After he had been in the water a few hours, seriously concerned about being captured by Japanese on Chichi Jima, Bush was rescued by the submarine *Finback.* Lieutenant White and Aviation Radioman John Delaney were killed in the operation; fate had spared Nadeau.

And Now the Trap

United States Navy

William S. Phillips

LATE IN THE WAR AND LATE IN THE DAY, THREE F6FS PREPARE TO ASSUME THE LANDING pattern and head back to the USS *Hornet*. The three fighters are part of Commander Ed Konrad's Air Group 17, which went aboard the carrier in February 1945.

This *Hornet*, which was commissioned in late November 1943, took the name of the earlier carrier that had launched Doolittle's raiders in April 1942 and was sunk in October of that year in the Solomons. The first commanding officer was the brilliant but irascible Captain Miles Browning, who had been Admiral Halsey's chief of staff on and off since the beginning of the war. In a 1986 *Naval Institute Proceedings* article titled "Death of a Captain," former dive-bomber pilot Hal Buell described the skipper's professional demise. Admiral Ernest King, the chief of naval operations in Washington, D.C., believed that Halsey needed a more stable chief of staff but knew that the loyal Halsey was loath to part with Browning. Halsey would let him go, however, to take a carrier command, so Browning was put in charge of the new *Hornet*, which would be Rear Admiral Jocko Clark's flagship. After a number of preventable mishaps onboard, including a hangar deck event that resulted in the death of a crew member, Browning was relieved of command.

The *Hornet* and her planes participated in actions as part of the the fast carrier task force from March 1944 onward: the Marianas, the Philippines, attacks on the Japanese home islands, Iwo Jima, and Okinawa. In April 1945 her planes joined in the savaging of the battleship *Yamato*, and on June 4–5 of that year she ran afoul of a ferocious Pacific typhoon that sent the forward edge of her flight deck drooping.

After a postwar stint in mothballs, the carrier was modernized considerably, serving first as an attack carrier and later as an antisubmarine platform. In the latter role, she also participated in the early years of the U.S. space program. After the Apollo 11 astronauts completed the first moon walks in July 1969, they returned to earth and were recovered by the *Hornet*. The ship is now preserved at Alameda, California, as a tourist attraction.

Imperial Sacrifice
United States Navy

Robert Bailey

AT SOME 70,000 TONS (63,503t) OF FULL-LOAD DISPLACEMENT AND ARMED WITH nine 18.1-inch (46cm) guns apiece, the Japanese *Yamato* and *Musashi* represented the ultimate in battleship development. The irony is that they entered fleet service shortly after the attack on Pearl Harbor, which had demonstrated conclusively that aircraft carriers had stolen the thunder from battleships as offensive weapons. In October 1944 the *Musashi* was overwhelmed by U.S. carrier-based bombers and torpedo planes and sunk in the Sibuyan Sea in the Battle of Leyte Gulf. The *Yamato* was part of the force that menaced the U.S. escort carriers and destroyers off Samar. She was the flagship of Vice Admiral Takeo Kurita, who turned back short of the beachhead and took the ships back to Japan—not having achieved their mission of foiling the invasion of Leyte.

By the next time the *Yamato* ventured forth, the Japanese fleet had largely ceased to be a factor in the war. The U.S. invasion of Okinawa on April 1, 1945, signified an ever nearer encroachment toward the Japanese home islands; Okinawa lay only 340 miles (547km) away. As a final defensive effort, the Japanese dispatched kamikaze aircraft in droves against the American invasion fleet, and the Imperial Navy had similar plans to sacrifice its largest warship. The *Yamato* steamed forth from the Inland Sea together with a light cruiser and eight destroyers. The objective of the one-way trip for the battleship was to beach herself on Okinawa and provide gunfire support for Japanese ground troops. Without the benefit of Japanese air cover, she didn't even get close. Admiral Raymond Spruance, a veteran surface-ship officer, was in command of the Fifth Fleet. He hoped that his battleships could take on the Japanese giant, but Admiral Mitscher's Task Force 58 was in a more propitious position. *Imperial Sacrifice* portrays the *Yamato*'s end, which came on the afternoon of April 7, 1945, as a swarm of nearly 400 planes—Corsair and Hellcat fighters, Helldiver bombers, and torpedo-laden Avengers—swooped down on the hapless dreadnought. She exploded and sank, taking with her approximately 2,500 Japanese sailors and bringing to an end the era of the super battleships. Also sunk were the cruiser *Yahagi* and four of the eight escorting destroyers.

Robert Bailey A.S.A.A. ©1998

Kamikaze

United States Navy

Dwight C. Shepler

BY THE AUTUMN OF 1944, AVAILABLE JAPANESE PILOTS WERE FAR FEWER AND FAR LESS skilled than the ones who had begun the war. With the U.S. invasion of Leyte in the Philippines, the Japanese were forced to take desperate measures as they attempted to defend their ever shrinking empire. Kamikaze suicide flights were a military strategy born of that desperation. In Japanese, *kamikaze* means "divine wind," referring to a sixteenth-century typhoon that scattered a Chinese fleet attempting to invade Japan. The World War II version of the kamikaze defense called for minimally trained Japanese pilots to fly bomb-laden aircraft toward the American fleet, attempt to penetrate antiaircraft defenses, and crash into the U.S. warships.

Kamikazes rammed into dozens of American warships, particularly during the Okinawa campaign in the spring of 1945. Picket destroyers took many hits, but so too did the carriers, which were vulnerable because their wood-covered flight decks were not armored. For the kamikazes, who were not trying to evade antiaircraft fire, the job was to ignore the flak and bear down on the target. The plane depicted in *Kamikaze* has done just that, turning itself into a guided missile in its approach to the *Hornet*'s deck.

Suicide planes damaged dozens of ships and took hundreds of lives, but the worst was avoided. Hundreds of planes had returned to Japan for the last-ditch defense of the home islands in the autumn of 1945. But the Japanese surrender on August 15 precluded their use and saved many lives on both sides. One who did not survive was Admiral Matome Ugaki, commander of the Fifth Air Fleet at the end of the war. He believed that he and his fellow Japanese should fight to the end rather than surrender; he felt an overpowering sense of shame when Emperor Hirohito proclaimed that it was time for them to lay down their arms. Ugaki drank a farewell cup of sake with his staff and then, together with a band of loyalists, set out on his own suicide mission, determined to crash into American ships at Okinawa. His plane and those accompanying him were lost at sea, short of their target. Afterward, Ugaki's aide found the last note left by the admiral: "Having a dream, I will go up into the sky."

The *Bunker Hill* burns after taking a hit by two kamikazes a few seconds apart on May 11, 1945. The attack cost the lives of nearly 400 men onboard the carrier.

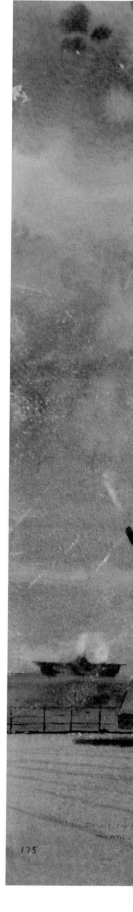

Corsair Recovery

British Royal Navy

Robert Taylor

IN 1944, AS THE FIGHTING IN EUROPE MOVED INLAND AND THE GERMAN NAVY POSED a far smaller threat than before, Great Britain pushed to get the Royal Navy into action in the Pacific theater. Admiral Ernie King, commander in chief of the U.S. Fleet, resisted this move because of a concern about logistical support for the ships in the far Pacific. In September 1944, at a meeting in Quebec, Canada, Allied leaders agreed that the British Pacific Fleet could operate with the Americans. British carrier planes, however, were woefully less capable than their American counterparts, so U.S. planes were supplied to the British, along with liaison officers to enable the combined fleets to follow standard U.S. procedures.

Rather than being intermingled with the U.S. carriers, the carriers of the British Pacific Fleet constituted a separate force—Task Force 57. Though smaller and slower than the U.S. carriers, the British ships had the advantage of armored flight decks as protection against kamikazes. During the lead-up to the Okinawa campaign in the spring of 1945, the British attacked Sakashima Gunto, a group of islands nearby, and that summer the British joined in air attacks on the Japanese home islands.

In *Corsair Recovery*, two Corsairs of the Fleet Air Arm are in the landing circuit, preparing to be recovered aboard HMS *Formidable* after a July 1945 attack against Japanese airfields and shipping. The pilot of the lead Corsair is Lieutenant Robert Gray. In August, Gray sank the Japanese escort ship *Amakusa*. Unfortunately, he perished in the encouter. For his heroic act, he was awarded a posthumous Victoria Cross.

General Quarters

United States Navy

William F. Draper

OPERATIONS AT SEA MEANT A FATIGUING ROUTINE FOR THE CREWS OF WARSHIPS IN TASK group operations. They stood watches around the clock, of course, with a schedule that often called for four hours on and eight off. Fitted into the eight off were regular shipboard work, eating, sleeping, washing, infrequent recreation—and general quarters. Crews often went to battle stations at dawn and dusk to provide maximum alertness at times when low visibility gave enemy submarines the opportunity to launch torpedo attacks virtually undetected. And when the carriers approached a target, as in this painting of the *Yorktown* during a strike against the Palau Islands, the men were summoned by the strident bonging of the general alarm and the passing of the word over the ship's public address system.

While at sea, defense against enemy aircraft was carried out in layers. The first line of defense came from fighter planes that operated on combat air patrol and attempted to intercept enemy aircraft before they came within range of the task group. The attack carriers generally operated in the center of a large, circular formation of ships. On the outer ring were destroyers to provide protection against both submarines and enemy aircraft. Closer in were cruisers and battleships, all sprouting forests of antiaircraft guns topside. The "leakers" that penetrated through all those layers came under fire from the carrier's own guns. Forward and aft of the island on the flight deck were 5-inch (13cm)/38-caliber twin mounts. The antiaircraft defenses along the outer edge of the flight deck on the port side are shown here in *General Quarters*. Visible are the large single barrels of the 5-inch (13cm) guns, which had the longest range. Closer are 40-millimeter guns, which were typically contained in quadruple mounts of two pairs. Not shown are the still smaller 20-millimeters, which had the shortest range.

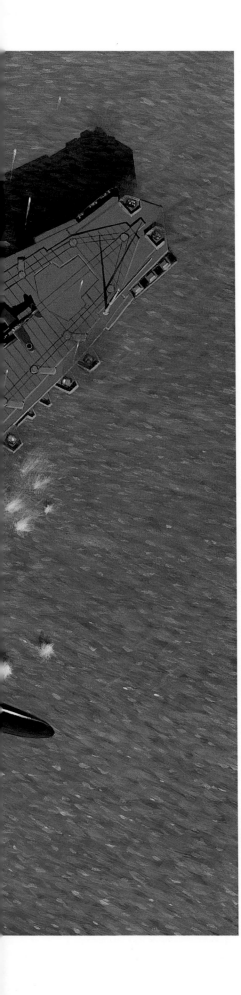

Big Tailed Beast
United States Navy

Stan Stokes

By the summer of 1945 the Imperial Japanese Navy had essentially gone into remission and retreat as American carrier planes attacked the home islands on a daily basis. On July 24 and 28, the Americans unleashed a series of strikes that rained destructive blows on the naval base at Kure on the Inland Sea of Japan. The Japanese did not mount an air defense because they were saving their planes for the invasion expected later that year. Among the victims of the late July attacks were the battleships *Ise, Hyuga*, and *Haruna*, and the heavy cruisers *Tone* and *Aoba*; several carriers were also damaged.

It was a reckoning that had been a long time coming, for the Japanese ships had been tormenting the Americans since the beginning of the war. When Admiral Halsey turned south at Leyte Gulf, he had reluctantly left behind a number of potential targets, including the hybrid battleship-carriers *Ise* and *Hyuga*. These two were originally completed as battleships during World War I; each mounted twelve 14-inch (36cm) guns, making them comparable to U.S. battleships of the era. In 1943–44, in an attempt to compensate for the carriers lost at Midway, the Japanese Navy removed the after turrets from the two ships and replaced them with hangars and short flight decks. The plan was to store and handle seaplane bombers that would be launched by catapults and recovered after landing in the water alongside the ship. But these seaplanes never materialized, so in October 1944 the catapults were removed to improve the arcs of fire for the remaining after turrets.

Big Tailed Beast presents a bird's-eye view as Lieutenant Paul "Flyboy" Brehm from Air Group 87 on the *Ticonderoga* takes a steep dive down into a torrent of antiaircraft tracer bullets; he chose not to deploy his dive brakes to minimize his exposure to the flak. He has just released a 1,000-pound (454kg) bomb aimed at the *Hyuga*. She took nearly a dozen hits, including Brehm's, plus many more near-misses. The old warship was so badly damaged by the day's strike that she filled up with water, settled to the bottom, and was abandoned by her crew. Four days later, planes from Task Force 38 sank her sister, *Ise*, not far away. These contemporaries of the *Arizona* would fight no more.

Topaz One at Twilight
United States Marine Corps

Brian Bateman

Major Bruce Porter and his Hellcat, "Black Death," at Yontan airfield, Okinawa, in 1945.

AS THE WAR IN THE PACIFIC ADVANCED, THE NAVY FELT AN INCREASING NEED FOR night carrier capability. Earlier in the Pacific campaign, the operations had been primarily conducted in daytime only; night landings generally occurred only in unexpected or emergency circumstances. But the Japanese could still pose a threat at night and had even sent up harassing planes during the Guadalcanal campaign to disturb the sleep of the fliers and Marines on the ground there. In November 1943, as noted earlier, Lieutenant Commander Butch O'Hare and his wingman had experimented with pioneering tactics by flying their Hellcats in tandem with a radar-equipped TBF Avenger. By 1944 the Hellcats themselves had acquired night capability with the installation of a radar pod under the leading edge of the right wing, and in 1944 the CVL *Independence* had become a specialized night carrier. Later, the *Enterprise*, which had pioneered night attack operations under Lieutenant Commander Bill Martin, was converted to night work as well. For the final months of the war, she and the *Independence* teamed up to form a night carrier division.

Marine Corps pilots also moved toward night capability. Major Bruce Porter was commanding officer of VMF(N)-542, Night Fighter Squadron 542. His radar-equipped Hellcat was armed with two 20-millimeter cannons and four .50-caliber machine guns. On the night of June 15, 1945, flying from Yontan airfield on Okinawa, he shot down two Japanese aircraft and a Baka suicide bomber. He was the only Marine pilot to achieve double kills in both the Corsair and the Hellcat. Porter had previously made some of the early night carrier landings. He is shown in *Topaz One at Twilight* piloting his F6F-5N, the night version of the Hellcat. Rare for carrier-type planes during the war, it has nose art in the form of the title "Black Death," which he christened his aircraft in honor of Schenley's whiskey. As dusk falls over Okinawa, Porter takes off to protect the anchored fleet from kamikazes. "Black Death" climbs to await the evening's assignment as another Hellcat banks toward its station.

Victory Flyover

United States Navy

Robert Taylor

IN MID-AUGUST 1945, AFTER ENDURING THE TWO U.S. ATOMIC BOMBS DROPPED ON ITS cities, Japan agreed to surrender. The war that had begun for the United States with the attack on Pearl Harbor had ended at last. It took a while to make arrangements for a formal surrender ceremony and to get U.S. occupation forces in place. With their vivid memories of the Japanese surprise attack in December 1941, the Americans were still not convinced that the surrender offer was completely in good faith. So when the victorious Allied warships steamed into Tokyo Bay in late August, one group of vessels was conspicuous by its absence—the American aircraft carriers. They remained outside the bay, ready to strike in case the Japanese tried to sabotage the surrender ceremony.

Admiral William Halsey rode in onboard his Third Fleet flagship, the battleship *Missouri*. On the way, someone asked him about the carriers, and he replied, "You know, I was writing a letter to my wife last night, and I told her, 'Well, dear, this is the day we have been looking forward to. I'm going into Tokyo Bay to accept the surrender terms of the Japs onboard the *Missouri*. You know why I'm aboard the *Missouri*? That's President Truman's home state, and President Truman's daughter christened the *Missouri*. But, you know, you don't have anything to worry about, dear. You're doing all right because I only brought one aircraft carrier into Tokyo Bay with me. That's the *Cowpens*, and that's the one that our daughter christened.'"

Once all the documents had been duly signed onboard the flagship on the morning of September 2, 1945, General of the Army Douglas MacArthur put his arm around Halsey's shoulder and whispered, "Start 'em now." With that, more than 450 Third Fleet carrier planes that had been orbiting nearby roared in over the ships anchored in Tokyo Bay. They were so low and so loud that they drowned out all conversation. It was an appropriate punctuation mark to conclude the surrender ceremony and a memorable demonstration of the carrier air power that had defeated Japan.

Saratoga

United States Navy

Tom Freeman

A cauliflower-shaped cloud of water vapor blossoms over the lagoon after an atomic bomb test at Bikini Atoll.

THE *SARATOGA* WAS THE U.S. NAVY'S SECOND AIRCRAFT carrier, commissioned in November 1927, about a month before her sister *Lexington*. The two converted battle cruisers played a vital role in preparing the United States to engage in carrier warfare so effectively in the Pacific some fifteen years later. Twice torpedoed, the *Saratoga* missed most of the major carrier battles during the pivotal year of 1942. When she did enter the fray, it was often in locations far removed from the center of action, because the old ship was not able to maneuver as nimbly as the newer carriers. She achieved a notable success in the Rabaul raid described earlier and contributed to operations with the British in the Indian Ocean.

With war's end in 1945, the old ship's duties as a plane carrier were over, but she became a giant transport and carried nearly 30,000 war veterans home from overseas. With that accomplished, she was expendable—the Navy now had far more new carriers than it could support in peacetime. She was designated as a target ship for tests at Bikini in the Marshall Islands in July 1946. There, a joint task force exploded two atomic bombs to determine their effect on warships. For the second blast, which took place on July 25, she was near the epicenter. Her large stack tumbled over, and she slowly disappeared from sight, sinking some 180 feet (55m) to the bottom of the lagoon. In 1988 and 1989, dive teams from the National Park Service explored the sunken remains. Diver/historian James Delgado prepared a report on her condition—it reads like an autopsy for a warship—that was published in the October 1990 issue of the Naval Institute's *Proceedings* magazine. Using underwater photos and descriptions provided by the divers, artist Tom Freeman created *Saratoga*, a portrait of the old warship's decomposing corpse. In what had once been an indentation on the starboard side for storing the ship's boats, a spot of yellow glows: the beam of a flashlight carried by the tiny frogman who peers into the long-abandoned interior. He sees only the marine life that now inhabits a ship where men once lived, worked, and helped build the U.S. carrier strike force.

About the Artists

C.S. Bailey's motto is "If it flies or floats I paint it!" Aviation and naval themes are his favorite subjects to draw and paint. Along with the paintbrush, he specializes in the use of the airbrush to help create his vividly rendered works. "What better way to paint aircraft than with air?" Bailey asks. Bailey earned a BFA in Fine Arts from the University of Utah and an MAED from the University of Phoenix. In addition to being the featured artist at the Salt Lake Aviation Aerospace Expo in 1994, Bailey's paintings have appeared in such publications as *Flight* and *Aviation History* magazines and, more recently, in a Tehabi and Time Life book on Pearl Harbor. He was among forty-seven Utah artists to be honored in the "Days of '47" art show and his paintings have hung at the Pensacola Naval Museum art show. C.S. Bailey is a member of the American Society of Aviation Artists and the Oklahoma Aviation Artist Association, and actively participates in the U.S. Air Force Art Program. But his greatest treasure and accomplishments are his four children and the support of his loving wife.

For information or to order prints:
C.S. Bailey Studios
2066 Greenbriar Circle
Salt Lake City, UT 84109
tel: (800) 494-6904

Even as a small boy, **Robert Bailey** was always drawing and painting aircraft. Born and raised in England, where he attended the College of Art in Stoke-on-Trent, Straffordshire, he was originally inspired by his father, who often told exciting tales of battles in North Africa and Italy. Most boys growing up in England in the shadows of World War II were avid readers of *Commando* comics, and Robert was no exception. He has amassed a large collection of these comics plus more than eighty books on the fictional fighter pilot "Biggles." He also owns an impressive library of books on military and aviation history, as well as a large collection of model airplanes that he uses as additional visual data. Bailey is an Artist Fellow with the American Society of Aviation Artists and a member of the Canadian Aviation Artists Association. His prints and originals are sold worldwide.

For information or to order prints:
Bailey Art and Publishing, Inc.
4 Brightbank Avenue
Stony Plain, Alberta, Canada T7Z 1G6
tel: (780) 963-5480
fax: (780) 963-7193
e-mail:bailart@telusplanet.net
www.telusplanet.net/public/bailart

Brian Bateman was born in Dayton, Ohio, in 1961. His interest in aviation began at the age of twelve; he would draw the artwork seen on model airplane boxes. From there he immersed himself in history, in particular aviation history. His constant need for information drives him toward getting the facts correct while being able to portray individual moments in time. Brian released his first lithograph in 1995, and since then has released numerous others to add to his inventory. He has clients around the world collecting his art, and is becoming well known for the dramatic moods that he portrays in each of his works. His special interests include Civil War and World War II history, aviation history, and hiking the great outdoors.

For information or to order prints:
Bateman Galleries
1697 Marbella Drive
Vista, CA 92083
tel: (760) 727-0154
e-mail:
Brian_Bateman@upperdeck.com

Born in New York in 1904, **Robert Benny** studied at some of the city's most prestigious art schools, such as the National Academy of Design, Cooper Union, and the Art Students League. Before his twentieth birthday, he had opened his own studio and begun a career as an illustrator for magazines and newspapers in the New York area. Later, he provided artistic commissions for major industries and companies. In 1943, he was hired to create paintings depicting the Naval Aviation Department's role in the crucial battles of the Pacific. In 1944, Benny was asked to document the Army Medical Department in the South Pacific. While there, he covered the invasions of Saipan and the Marianas. In 1954, the Society of Illustrators, of which Benny was a part, volunteered its services to the U.S. Air Force. In 1968, he again offered his services as a war correspondent and served with the Marines in Vietnam. Between his stints as a war correspondent, Benny worked on illustrations for major American companies and industrial associations. He taught at Pratt Institute from 1949 to 1952, and was Associate Professor of Fine and Commercial Art at Dutchess County College from 1964 to 1973. His works are now displayed by all branches of the armed services, and housed in the permanent collections of the Smithsonian Institute, the Dallas Museum of Fine Arts, the Corcoran Gallery of Art, and other distinguished organizations.

For information or to order prints:
Naval Historical Foundation—Photo Service
1306 Dahlgren Avenue SE, Washington Navy Yard
Washington, DC 20374-5055
tel: 202-678-4311
fax: 202-889-3565
e-mail: nhfhistsvc@aol.com
www.mil.org/navyhist/

Originally from Great Britain and now residing in New York, **Mark Churms** has quickly risen to the top of his profession. He began his career as an artist in 1991 by publishing his exemplary works with the well known military prints firm Cranston Fine Arts in Scotland, and then moved to the United States to become Vice President of TheHistoryWeb.com. Churms is now his own boss and publishes his own prints. Realism, detail, accuracy, dramatic lighting, and strong compositions are the reasons why many military collectors and enthusiasts agree that he is among the world's premier historical artists working today.

While many history artists paint a limited range of subject matter—such as aviation art, American Civil War, Naval battles, historical buildings, or portraits—Churms has lent his brush to a huge diversity of historical subject matter covering a wide range of eras. His skill in portraying land, sea, and air combat has earned him admiration, acclaim, and a huge following of military collectors interested in diverse periods of military history. Mark Churms' art can be seen in military museums, art galleries, and at specialist picture-framers worldwide. His original art has been exhibited at a variety of prestigious locations, including Christie's and Sotheby's in London, the Household Cavalry Museum in Windsor, and the Bannockburn Heritage Center in Scotland.

For information or to order prints:
e-mail: info@markchurms.com
www.markchurms.com

For **James Dietz**, simply illustrating aviation hardware is not presenting the whole picture; he prefers to add a human element to truly capture the moment in his paintings. "The people, settings, and costumes are what make aviation history exciting and romantic to me," says the artist. A graduate of the Art Center College of Design, he worked as a commercial illustrator in Los Angeles before moving to Seattle to pursue a career in aviation art. His clients include Boeing, Bell Helicopter, Allison, and the Flying Tigers. His work has been voted Best in Show in three successive years in the Experimental Aircraft Association Aviation Art Show, Best in Show four times for Flying Magazine/Simuflite Aviation Art Show, twice Best in Show for the Naval Aviation Museum Art Show, and he has been awarded the R.G. Smith Award for Excellence in Naval Aviation Art. His work has been exhibited in museums throughout the country, including the Experimental Aircraft Association Museum, the San Diego Air Museum, and the Smithsonian Institution's National Air and Space Museum.

For more information or to order prints:
James Dietz
2203 13th Avenue East
Seattle, WA 98102
tel: (206) 325-1151
fax: (206) 325-1151
e-mail:dietzart@aol.com

Lieutenant Commander **William Franklin Draper** was born in Hopedale, Massachusetts, in 1912. His practiced his art at Pomfret School in Connecticut and then at Harvard University. From there he went on to The National Academy of Design in New York and the Cape Art School in Massachusetts. In 1942, Draper was commissioned as a Lieutenant JG in the Naval Reserve, and was later sent to Alaska, where he spent six months in the Aleutian Island Chain. He was present at the Japanese attack on Amchitka Island and depicted the event in paintings. In creating this series of paintings he ran into difficulties peculiar to the climate of the Aleutian Islands, such as eccentric winds blowing his canvas into the air and arctic chills that made painting possible only while wearing gloves to keep his hands from freezing. After his return from Alaska he was designated to paint the portrait of Rear Admiral J.R. Beardall, the Superintendent of the Naval Academy. Upon completion of the portrait he was assigned to the Pacific where he painted various naval activities at Noumea and other bases. He was commissioned to paint the Portraits of Admiral Chester W. Nimitz and Admiral William F. Halsey. For his services in the Pacific, Draper was awarded the Bronze Star. He left the service in October 1945 after obtaining the rank of Lieutenant Commander. He then returned to his career as a painter, becoming one of the premiere portrait painters in America. Some of his subjects included John F. Kennedy (1962), the Shah of Iran (1967), James Michener (1979), and Richard M. Nixon (1981).

For information or to order prints:
Naval Historical Foundation—Photo Service
1306 Dahlgren Avenue SE, Washington Navy Yard
Washington, DC 20374-5055
tel: (202) 678-4311
fax: (202) 889-3565
e-mail: nhfhistsvc@aol.com
www.mil.org/navyhist/

Carl Gottfried Evers was born in Germany and spent much of his childhood in that country. He later moved to Great Britain, where he studied advertising art with a printing firm before attending the Slade School of Art at the University of London. After winning numerous awards and establishing his career as an artist, Evers moved to Sweden, and spent sixteen years honing his craft by creating illustrations for major automotive manufacturers. Determined to paint marine subjects, he moved to the United States in 1947, choosing to make the trip by boat so that he could observe the movements and moods of the sea, a decision that taught him a great deal about painting seascapes and waves. In New York, he painted for shipping companies and later illustrated covers and provided inside art for such publications as *Reader's Digest* and *Proceedings*, the U.S. Naval Institute's official magazine. This art was reproduced on a large scale, leading Evers' prints to be displayed in more than fifty thousand homes and businesses, and allowing him to continue creating privately commissioned works of art. In 1975, *The Marine Art of Carl G. Evers* was published, and in 1988 he was honored by the U.S. Naval Institute for twenty-six years of artistic contribution. He died on June 19, 2000, in Middlebury, Connecticut, at the age of ninety-two.

For information or to order prints:
Sturges & Mathes
Heritage Village
574 Heritage Road
P.O. Box 808
Southbury, CT 06488-0808
tel: (203) 264-8225
fax: (203) 262-6542

Tom Freeman has devoted his career to translating historical accounts into images. His historical and educational paintings have been featured in hundreds of books and magazines and can be found in galleries worldwide. Since 1986, many of his paintings have graced the walls of the west wing of the White House. To commemorate the December 7, 1941, attack on Pearl Harbor, Freeman produced a collection of forty-two paintings now on permanent exhibit at the Arizona Memorial in Honolulu. He has also just recently exhibited twelve paintings at the Naval Museum in Washington, D.C., to commemorate the sixtieth anniversary of the Pearl Harbor attack. One of Freeman's paintings was donated to the State of Israel, where it hangs in the Immigration/Clandestine and Naval Museum in Haifa. Freeman's work has been exhibited at the Navy Museum, the Naval Academy Museum, and the National Air and Space Museum. In 2002, His Eminence William Cardinal Keeler, Archbishop of Baltimore, will present one of Freeman's paintings to Pope John Paul II. The painting, entitled *Ship of State*, depicts the first visit of a Pope to U.S. territory on board the USS *Constitution* in Gaeta, Italy, in 1848. Tom Freeman's concern for authenticity and exacting detail has won him acclaim from art and historical communities worldwide.

For more information or to order prints:
SM&S Naval Prints, Inc.
1251 Bonaire Road PO Box 41
Forest Hill, MD 21050
tel: (410) 893-8184
fax: (410) 879-1261
e-mail:
TATSSEB@worldnet.net.ATT.NET

One of the nation's leading watercolor artists, **Mitchell Jamieson** was born in Kensington, Maryland, and attended the Abbott School of Fine and Commercial Arts and the Corcoran School of Art in Washington, D.C. Having already established himself with many noted commissions, he began his duty in 1942 as an official Combat Artist depicting the Navy and its various operations, from the North African campaigns to the South Pacific. During World War II, he was awarded the Bronze Star by the Navy, and his combat paintings were later reproduced extensively in *Life*, *Fortune*, and other national publications. Of his Navy combat art experience, Jamieson remarked, "I've confined my painting to what I have experienced and know to be strictly true, at the same time having to adapt my way of working to the pressure of time and swift-moving events. Yet anything that is worthwhile or that has the bite of reality in the work produced under these circumstances probably derives from a constant effort to share as fully as possible in the lives and experiences of others." Twice awarded the Guggenheim Fellowship and the Award of Merit by the American Academy of Arts and Letters, Jamieson died in 1976.

For more information or to order prints:
Naval Historical Foundation—Photo Service
1306 Dahlgren Avenue SE, Washington Navy Yard
Washington, DC 20374-5055
tel: (202) 678-4311
fax: (202) 889-3565
e-mail: nhfhistsvc@aol.com
www.mil.org/navyhist/

Craig Kodera has always loved aviation. Born in Riverside, California, in 1956, he cannot remember a time when airplanes and flight were not a part of his life. Kodera was raised in what he calls an "aviation family," in a neighborhood very close to the Los Angeles Airport. He was quick to pursue his dreams of art and aviation: he started to paint at age fourteen and, by the time he was seventeen, had earned his private pilot's license. Kodera attended UCLA, serving in the Air Force ROTC for three of his four years there. After graduation, he worked as a commercial artist, and also for McDonnell-Douglas Aircraft. Art and aviation merged at McDonnell-Douglas, and Kodera found himself employed as a production/design artist and illustrator. He later spent more than seven years in the Air Force Reserves, and after completing OTS and flight training, was assigned to the Air Rescue Service, logging over 1,300 flying hours in the Lockheed HC-130H Hercules.

Today, Kodera flies for American Airlines. Despite his often hectic schedule, he has always found time for his fine art. He has been with the Greenwich Workshop since 1984, and is the Charter Vice President of the American Society of Aviation Artists, as well as being a member of the Air Force Art Program. His work hangs in several museums and is part of the permanent collection of the Smithsonian Institution's National Air and Space Museum. He was the winner of the R.G. Smith "Excellence in Naval Aviation Art" award in 2001, and has won other top honors in prestigious aviation art competitions.

For more information or to order prints:
The Greenwich Workshop
One Greenwich Place
PO Box 875
Shelton, CT 06484
tel: (800) 243-4246

Tom Lea, an artist and writer whose work was praised by President George W. Bush in his acceptance speech at the Republican National Convention in August 2000, was initially a landscape painter. He produced murals for public buildings in Dallas and El Paso, Texas, and for the Benjamin Franklin Post Office in Washington, D.C. During World War II, Lea worked as an illustrator and war correspondent in the Pacific for *Life* magazine. He also illustrated *The Longhorns*, a book by Frank Dobie, and wrote several books himself, including *The Wonderful Country* and *The Brave Bulls*, both of which were made into movies in the 1950s, and *A Picture Gallery*. His artworks are included in the collection of the Smithsonian Institute. Tom Lea died in 2001 at the age of ninety-three.

For more information or to order prints:
U.S. Army Center of Military History
DAMH-MDC Building 35
103 Third Street
Fort Lesley J. McNair, DC 20319-5056
tel: (202) 761-5373
fax: (202) 761-5444

Upon graduating from the College of Fine Arts at Syracuse University, **Albert K. Murray**, a native of Emporia, Kansas, continued pursuing his artistic studies in the United States and abroad. Already a renowned portrait painter before he was commissioned a Lieutenant with the Combat Art Section of the Navy, his first official assignment was to create a series of portraits of the Navy's General Board. This was the first of his many noted military portraits. With the Fourth Fleet, South Atlantic, and then the Eighth Fleet, North African waters, he often sketched in the heat of battle. After the war, and having been awarded the Bronze Star for bravery, Murray painted official portraits of Navy war heroes for the service and served as the director of the Navy Combat Art Collection and its Operation Palette. As a civilian, he painted prominent non-military individuals, among them Thomas J. Watson of IBM, the philanthropist Laurance S. Rockefeller, and Arthur Hays Sulzberger, former publisher of *The New York Times*. His work is represented in the collections of the National Gallery of Art, the National Portrait Gallery, the National Museum of American Art, and the U.S. Departments of Commerce, Treasury, and Justice. Albert K. Murray died in 1992.

For more information or to order prints:
Naval Historical Foundation—Photo Service
1306 Dahlgren Avenue SE, Washington Navy Yard
Washington, DC 20374-5055
tel: (202) 678-4311
fax: (202) 889-3565
e-mail: nhfhistsvc@aol.com
www.mil.org/navyhist/

For as long as he can remember, **Bill Phillips** has had a love affair with flight, and his aviation art conveys his passion to the viewer. Phillips has logged hours in F-106s, F-15s, and RF-4s, and has spent a tour of duty in the Air Force, including an assignment at Tan Son Nhut, Vietnam. There he spent many afternoons sketching the various aircraft on the base and the beautiful clouds that would gather during the monsoon season. Phillips' work hangs in numerous public and private collections throughout the world. In June of 1987 he was given a one-man retrospective at the National Air and Space Museum in Washington, D.C.—one of only a few artists to be so honored. The show was so popular that it toured North America for four years. In 1991 and 2000, Phillips' works received the "History Award" as part of "Art for the Parks," the prestigious annual fund-raiser for the National Park Service. And, in July of 1997, the U.S. Postal Service released a twenty-stamp sheet depicting "Classic American Aircraft" that Phillips had been commissioned to paint.

For more information or to order prints:
William S. Phillips Fine Art
P.O. Box 677
Ashland, OR 97520
tel: (541) 482-8093
fax: (541) 482-1157

Born in 1930 in Cincinnati, Ohio, **Hugh Polder** attended night school at the Central Academy of Commercial Art and the Gephart School of Portrait Painting. He enlisted in the Air Force from 1951–54 as illustrator for the 3300th Publication Unit Air Training Command, St. Louis, Missouri. After leaving the service, he became a commercial artist for studios and agencies. Polder started to freelance in the mid-1960s, illustrating catalogs, books, magazines, model covers, and calendars. He now specializes in historical aviation and marine art, inspired by his childhood near Lunken Airport and the Ohio River where, during World War II, he saw many LSTs, mine sweepers, etc. A resident of Chicago for forty years, Polder has donated paintings to the Air Force Art Program and the Experimental Aircraft Museum. His prints and paintings are exhibited in galleries around the country and his commission works and prints are sold around the world. He is also a member of the U.S. Naval Institute & American Society of Aviation Artists.

For more information or to order prints:
Hugh's Aviation Prints
3540 W. Beach Ave
Chicago, IL 60651-2201
tel: (773) 772-7683

John D. Shaw has pursued his art and graphics career since 1985. Born in 1961, this native of Carson City, Nevada, has always maintained an interest in creating both fine and commercial art. As an illustrator, Shaw has created artwork for a variety of clients, including Lucasfilms Ltd., Kellogg's, and Major League Baseball. Shaw's work took on a new emphasis in 1993, when he began creating paintings with an historical aviation theme. Paying special attention to the World War II era, his depictions of these aircraft, pilots, crews, and their missions have won national awards and have been included in a number of related publications, such as *Flying*, *Aviation History*, *World War II*, and *Military History*. To date, thirteen of his paintings have been reproduced as limited-edition lithographs, all of which are hand-signed by Shaw and famous aviators like Chennault's Flying Tigers, the Doolittle Tokyo Raiders, the Black Sheep Squadron, the Tuskegee Airman, the Mercury Astronauts, and others. The biography of General Gunther Rall of Germany, the world's highest scoring living fighter ace, features Shaw's paintings and illustrations throughout.

For more information or to order prints:
Liberty Studios
321 Secret Way Court
Casselberry, FL 32707
tel: (888) 893-3786
fax: (407) 265-0260

Born in Everett, Massachusetts, and a graduate of Williams College, **Dwight Shepler** became a member of the American Artists' Group and the American Artists Professional League. Commissioned in the Navy in May 1942 and assigned to the Combat Art Section, he first traveled with a destroyer on Pacific convoy duty. From the mud of Guadalcanal through the years of the Allied build-up in England to the memorable D-Day on the French Coast, Shepler painted and recorded all facets of naval warfare. For his service as a Combat Artist, the Navy awarded him the Bronze Star. After World War II, Shepler continued his career as a pioneer watercolorist of the high ski country, and served as president of the Guild of Boston Artists. Shepler died in 1974.

For more information or to order prints:
Naval Historical Foundation—Photo Service
1306 Dahlgren Avenue SE, Washington Navy Yard
Washington, DC 20374-5055
tel: (202) 678-4311
fax: (202) 889-3565
e-mail: nhfhistsvc@aol.com
www.mil.org/navyhist/

Thomas Skinner, who spent his childhood in North Carolina painting mountain scenery, studied art extensively in New York and Spain. In 1914 he was married, and in 1932 was named Staff Artist for the Mariners Museum in Virginia. In 1948, Skinner was the guest of the commanding officer of the carrier *Coral Seas* on a venture to the Mediterranean and the West Indies. As a result of this cruise, Skinner created two paintings for which he received much acclaim, one of the *Coral Seas* escorted by a destroyer and another of the battleship *Missouri* passing the Rock of Gibraltar. In that same year, a special exhibition of sixty of his paintings opened at the Mariners Museum. Thomas Skinner died in 1955 at the age of sixty-six.

For more information or to order prints:
The Mariners' Museum
Photographic Services & Licensing
100 Museum Drive
Newport News, VA 23606-3759
tel: (757) 591-7768
fax: (757) 591-7354

Born in 1914 in Los Angeles, California, **R.G. Smith** developed an early affinity for aviation, inspired by Charles Lindbergh's solo crossing of the Atlantic Ocean in 1927. Beginning his career as an engineer with Douglas Aircraft, Smith helped design such classic naval aircraft as the SBD Dauntless, AD Skyraider, A-3D Skywarrior, F-4D Skyray, and his personal favorite, the A-4D Skyhawk. At the same time, he was also developing a reputation as a respected artist, using his knowledge of airplane construction and function to give life to the aircraft in his artworks. After two tours as a Combat Artist in Vietnam and trips to naval units throughout the world, he was designated an "Honorary Naval Aviator," a distinction awarded to few civilians. His paintings and prints can now be found in museums and private collections alike, on naval vessels, the walls of the Pentagon, countless military installations, and congressional and corporate offices. Smith died on May 29, 2001.

For more information or to order prints:
#32 Hilton Head Drive
Rancho Mirage, CA 92270
tel: (760) 770-1966
fax: (760) 770-0092
e-mail: SharlynMarsh@aol.com

For more than twenty-five years, **Stan Stokes** has been depicting the world's greatest aircraft. Stokes' attention to detail and his superb illustrative techniques, especially his gift for creating three-dimensional effects, have made a name for the California artist. "Incredibly accurate" is a common description of a Stokes painting. His talent not going unnoticed, he received the Benedictine Art Award and first place in the Smithsonian Institute's National Air and Space Museum Golden Age of Flight Art Competition in 1984. His original paintings adorn many of the nation's most famous aviation museums, including the National Air and Space Museum, the Air Force Museum in Dayton, Ohio, and the Museum of Naval Aviation in Pensacola, Florida. From 1985–1991, he produced fourteen paintings for NASA's art collection. In 2000, Stokes was presented the R.G. Smith Award for Excellence in Naval Aviation Art by the National Museum of Naval Aviation Foundation, and in 2001 he finished a large mural of the Tuskegee Airmen, now at Palm Springs Air Museum.

For information or to order prints:
The Stokes Collection
26352 Carmel Rancho Lane, Suite 105
Carmel, CA 93923
tel: (800) 359-4644

Robert Taylor has been painting and sketching since his early years and has earned a reputation that makes him one of today's leading marine and aviation artists. His true talent lies in his ability to take viewers right into a scene, making it almost possible to smell the smoke of battle or to experience the exhilaration of flight and the movement of the sea. In the mid-1970s, a noteworthy alliance with the Military Gallery led Taylor on his path to fame. His clients have included the British royal family, a former American president, legendary pilots and aircrews, and countless other aviation and maritime enthusiasts. His work has been featured on television programs and in newspaper and magazine articles. *The Washington Post* described his paintings and drawings as exuding "a lyrical and majestic quality." His one-man exhibition in London in 1983 was heavily covered by international media, as was his one-man exhibition at the Smithsonian Institution's National Air and Space Museum in Washington, D.C., seen by ten million visitors. The latter has been quoted as the most successful aviation art exhibit ever staged. Today Taylor is the most collected aviation and marine artist in the world.

For information or to order prints:
Military Gallery/Universal Publishing Group
821 E. Ojai Avenue
Ojai, CA 93023
tel: (805) 640-0057
fax: (805) 640-0059
e-mail: milgallery@aol.com
www.militarygallery.com

Arriving on the scene in the late 1980s, **Nicolas Trudgian** is today a best-selling aviation and military artist, and has generated artwork for some of the major auto and aerospace manufacturers. Described as a landscape artist who paints aircraft, he enjoys painting the machinery of yesteryear with brilliant colors and resolution. Upon joining the Military Gallery in the late 1980s, his paintings were produced as prints for the first time, launching his successful career on an international scale. Today, the quality of his work is recognized around the globe, making him one of the most popular aviation and military artists in the world.

For information or to order prints:
Military Gallery/Universal Publishing Group
821 E. Ojai Avenue
Ojai, CA 93023
tel: (805) 640-0057
fax: (805) 640-0059
e-mail: milgallery@aol.com
www.militarygallery.com

Ted Wilbur is a naval aviator, combat artist, editor, and writer with more than thirty years of experience. His paintings hang in the National Air and Space Museum in Washington, D.C., and are a part of the U.S. Navy's permanent collection of art. Many of his works are also owned by private collectors. Designated a Naval Aviator in 1950, Captain Ted Wilbur experienced his first flying assignments in night fighter and attack squadrons. He served in VX-3 (Special Weapons) and in VS-26, and was a plank owner in VRC-40, the first designated COD squadron. He was officer in charge of fight support missions in the *Mercury* project. Additionally, his broad experience in carrier operations includes a total of more than six hundred landings aboard thirty-six aircraft carriers, and more than 5,000 hours in both single- and multi-engine aircraft. Wilbur had additional assignments as a Navy Combat Artist covering Projects *Vanguard* and *Polaris*, the manned space program, and nuclear submarines. His paintings and articles have appeared in both military and civilian magazines—*Naval Institute Proceedings*, *Time*, *True Magazine*, and *Saturday Review*.

For more information or to order prints:
Ted Wilbur
6821 Lemon Road
McLean, VA 22101
tel: (703) 893-8267

After initially pursuing a career in technical illustration and graphic design, **Keith Woodcock** decided in 1982 to devote his energies and talents to painting aviation subjects fulltime. Since then, he has become one of the most respected artists in his field, exhibiting widely in the United Kingdom, Europe, and North America. His work has won many awards, including a Par Excellence award at the EAA Aviation Art Competition in Oshkosh, Wisconsin, the prestigious Aviation Painting of the Year award at the guild of Aviation Artist's annual London exhibition (followed by the Best Oil Painting award at the same show three years later), the James V. Roy award at the annual American Society of Aviation Artist's exhibition, and an ASAA Award of Merit in 1999. Woodcock's paintings have received critical acclaim for their atmosphere and authenticity, the latter often demanding extensive research. Many examples of his artwork now hang in the permanent collections of museums, service establishments, aerospace companies, and private individuals worldwide. Virtually all his work is now specially commissioned.

For more information or to order prints:
Keith Woodcock
2nd floor, Adelphi Mill
Grimshaw Lane
Bollington, Macclesfield
SK10 5JB
England
e-mail: info@keithwoodcock.com
www.keithwoodcock.com

Bibliography

Books
Baldwin, Hanson W. *The Navy at War: Paintings and Drawings by Combat Artists*. New York: William Morrow and Company, 1943.

Ballard, Robert D., and Rick Archbold. *Return to Midway*. Washington: National Geographic Society and Madison Press, 1999.

Barde, Robert E. *The Battle of Midway: A Study in Command*. College Park: University of Maryland, 1972.

Buell, Harold L. *Dauntless Helldivers*. New York: Orion Books, 1991.

Cantrell, Bill. *Friends, Dear Friends, and Heroes: A Nostalgic Memoir of a WWII Marine Fighter Pilot*. Springfield, Missouri: Freebooter Publishing Company, 1997.

Carter, Worrall R. *Beans, Bullets, and Black Oil: The Story of Fleet Logistics Afloat in the Pacific During World War II*. Washington: Department of the Navy, 1953.

Chesnau, Roger, ed. *Conway's All the World's Fighting Ships: 1922–1946*. New York: Mayflower Books, 1980.

Cressman, Robert J. *That Gallant Ship: U.S.S. Yorktown (CV-5)*. Missoula, Montana: Pictorial Histories Publishing Co., 1985.

Cressman, Robert J. *"A Magnificent Fight": The Battle for Wake Island*. Annapolis: Naval Institute Press, 1995.

Cutler, Thomas J. *The Battle of Leyte Gulf, 23–26 October, 1944*. New York: HarperCollins, 1994.

Dull, Paul S. *A Battle History of the Imperial Japanese Navy (1941–1945)*. Annapolis: Naval Institute Press, 1978.

Engen, Donald D. *Wings and Warriors: My Life as a Naval Aviator*. Washington: Smithsonian Institution Press, 1997.

Ewing, Steve. *USS Enterprise (CV-6): The Most Decorated Ship of World War II*. Missoula, Montana: Pictorial Histories Publishing Company, 1982 (subsequently updated).

Ewing, Steve, and John B. Lundstrom. *Fateful Rendezvous: The Life of Butch O'Hare*. Annapolis: Naval Institute Press, 1997.

Fry, John. *USS Saratoga CV-3: An Illustrated History of the Legendary Aircraft Carrier, 1927–1946*. Atglen, Pennsylvania: Schiffer Publishing, 1996.

Galvin, John, with Frank Allnutt. *Salvation for a Doomed Zoomie*. Indian Hills, Colorado: Allnutt Publishing, 1983.

Gay, George H. *Sole Survivor: The Battle of Midway and its Effects on His Life*. Naples, Florida: Midway Publishers, 1980.

Goldstein, Donald M., and Katherine Dillon, eds. *Fading Victory: The Diary of Admiral Matome Ugaki, 1941–1945*. Pittsburgh: University of Pittsburgh Press, 1991.

Halsey, William F., Jr., with J. Bryan. *Admiral Halsey's Story*. New York: McGraw-Hill, 1947.

Honan, William H. *Visions of Infamy: The Untold Story of How Journalist Hector C. Bywater Devised the Plans that Led to Pearl Harbor*. New York: St. Martin's Press, 1991.

Hone, Thomas C., Norman Friedman, and Mark D. Mandeles. *American & British Aircraft Carrier Development: 1919–1941*. Annapolis: Naval Institute Press, 1999.

Hyams, Joe. *Flight of the Avenger: George Bush at War*. San Diego: Harcourt Brace Jovanovich, 1991.

Johnston, Stanley. *Queen of the Flat-Tops: The U.S.S. Lexington and the Coral Sea Battle*. New York: E.P. Dutton & Co., 1942.

Jentschura, Hansgeorg, Dieter Jung, and Peter Mickel. *Warships of the Imperial Japanese Navy, 1869–1945*. Annapolis: Naval Institute Press, 1977.

Kennedy, Ludovic. *Pursuit: The Chase and Sinking of the Battleship Bismarck*. New York: Viking Press, 1974.

Lord, Walter. *Incredible Victory*. New York: Harper & Row, 1967.

Lundstrom, John B. *The First Team and the Guadalcanal Campaign: Naval Fighter Combat from August to November, 1942*. Annapolis: Naval Institute Press, 1994.

Lundstrom, John B. *The First Team: Pacific Naval Air Combat from Pearl Harbor to Midway*. Annapolis: Naval Institute Press, 1984.

Mason, John T., Jr., ed. *The Pacific War Remembered: An Oral History Collection*. Annapolis: Naval Institute Press, 1986.

Morison, Samuel Eliot. *History of United States Naval Operations in World War II*. 15 vols. Boston: Little, Brown, 1947–1962.

Mullenheim-Rechberg, Baron Burkhard von. *Battleship Bismarck: A Survivor's Story*. Translated by Jack Sweetman. Annapolis: Naval Institute Press, 1980.

Park, Edwards. *The Art of William S. Phillips: The Glory of Flight*. Greenwich: The Greenwich Workshop, Inc., 1994.

Pawlowski, Gareth L. *Flat-tops and Fledglings: A History of American Aircraft Carriers*. South Brunswick, New York: A.S. Barnes and Co., 1971.

Polmar, Norman. *Aircraft Carriers: A Graphic History of Carrier Aviation and its Influence on World Events*. New York: Doubleday & Company, 1969.

Reynolds, Clark G. *Famous American Admirals*. New York: Van Nostrand Reinhold, 1978.

Reynolds, Clark G. *The Fast Carriers: The Forging of an Air Navy*. New York: McGraw Hill Book Company, 1968; Annapolis: Naval Institute Press, 1992.

Sakai, Saburo, with Martin Caidin and Fred Saito. *Samurai!* New York: Dutton, 1957; Annapolis: Naval Institute Press, 1991.

Shalett, Sidney. *Old Nameless: The Epic of a U.S. Battlewagon*. New York: D. Appleton Century, 1943.

Sherrod, Robert. *History of Marine Corps Aviation in World War II*. San Rafael, California: Presidio Press, 1980.

Stafford, Edward P. *The Big E*. New York: Random House, 1962.

Stillwell, Paul. *Air Raid: Pearl Harbor! Recollections of a Day of Infamy*. Annapolis: Naval Institute Press, 1981.

Stinnett, Robert B. *George Bush and His World War II Years*. Washington: Brassey's Inc., 1992.

Swanborough, Gordon, and Peter M. Bowers. *United States Navy Aircraft since 1911*. Annapolis: Naval Institute Press, 1976.

Sweetman, Jack. *American Naval History: An Illustrated Chronology of the U.S. Navy and Marine Corps 1775–Present*. Annapolis: Naval Institute Press, 1984 and 1991.

Taylor, Theodore. *The Magnificent Mitscher*. New York: Norton, 1954; Annapolis: Naval Institute Press, 1991.

Tillman, Barrett. *Corsair: The F4U in World War II and in Korea*. Annapolis: Naval Institute Press, 1979.

Tillman, Barrett. *The Dauntless Dive Bomber of World War Two*. Annapolis: Naval Institute Press, 1976.

Tillman, Barrett. *Hellcat, the F6F in World War II*. Annapolis: Naval Institute Press, 1979.

Watts, Anthony J., and Brian G. Gordon. *The Imperial Japanese Navy*. London: MacDonald & Company, 1971.

Wooldridge, E.T., ed. *Carrier Warfare in the Pacific: An Oral History Collection*. Washington: Smithsonian Institution Press, 1993.

Y'Blood, William T. *Hunter-Killer: U.S. Escort Carriers in the Battle of the Atlantic*. Annapolis: Naval Institute Press, 1983.

Articles
Buell, Harold L. "Death of a Captain." *U.S. Naval Institute Proceedings* (February 1986): 92–96.

Ferrier, H.H. "Torpedo Squadron Eight, the Other Chapter." *U.S. Naval Institute Proceedings* (October 1964): 72–76.

Greeley, Brendan. "Paso por Aqui: An Afternoon with Tom Lea." *Naval History* (April 1995): 8–17.

Ramsey, Logan C. "Aerial Attacks on Fleets at Anchor." *U.S. Naval Institute Proceedings* (August 1937): 1126–1132.

Sweetman, Jack. "Taranto." *Naval History*, (May/June 1995): 14–15. (This entire issue contains a series of twenty-one summaries of the major naval battles of World War II.)

"Tom Lea Aboard the U.S.S. 'Hornet.'" *Life* (March 11, 1943): 49.

Index

Photo Credits

©C.S. Bailey: 20, 21, 22

©Robert Bailey: 126–127

©Brian Bateman: 134–135

©Robert Benny: 83

©Mark Churms: 112

Corbis: 92; Bettmann, 49, 64, 114, 138

©James Dietz: Front Endpapers, 14–15, 18–19,
66–67, 72–73, 113

©William F. Draper: 87, 95, 96, 99, 107, 131

Courtesy of Charles Engen: 106, 116

Courtesy of the Estate of Carl G. Evers: 114–115

©Tom Freeman: 16, 88–89, 100–101, 116–117,
138–139; Courtesy of Arizona Memorial Museum
Association, Pearl Harbor Collection, 36–37, 38, 39

Courtesy of George Bush Presidential Library: 123

©Mitchell Jamieson: 93

©Craig Kodera: 2–3, 58–59, 68–69, 90–91, Back
Endpapers

©Tom Lea/ Courtesy of Army Art Collection, U.S.
Center of Military History: 74, 74–75, 78,
79 (all)

©Takeshi Maeda / Courtesy of David Aiken: 41

©Albert K. Murray: 104

National Archives: 23, 24–25, 46, 52, 57, 63 top,
63 bottom, 82, 84, 97, 98, 102, 109, 128; Courtesy of
Robert J. Cressman, 94; Courtesy of John Fry, 91;
Courtesy of Michael Green, 13 left, 13 right; Courtesy
of Kevin Ullrich, 101

Courtesy of National Museum of Naval Aviation:
12 left, 12 right, 13 top

©William S. Phillips: 6–7, 60–61, 62, 124–125

©Hugh Polder: 47, 120–121

Courtesy of R. Bruce Porter: 135

©John D. Shaw: 44–45, 48–49

©Dwight C. Shepler: 76–77, 128–129

©Thomas C. Skinner / Courtesy of The Mariners'
Museum: 15, 34–35

©R.G. Smith: 42–43, 55, 64–65, 110–111

©Stan Stokes: 8, 32–33, 40, 53, 56–57, 84–85,
132–133

©Robert Taylor/ Military Gallery: 28–29, 30–31,
50–51, 80–81, 104–105, 130, 136–137

©Nicolas Trudgian/ Military Gallery: 102–103

©Ted Wilbur: 24, 70, 71, 108–109, 118–119,
122–123

©Keith Woodcock: 26–27